THE
Emotional
Abuse
Recovery
WORKBOOK

THE
Emotional
Abuse
Recovery
WORKBOOK

Breaking the Cycle of Psychological Violence

THERESA COMITO, LMFT

ROCKRIDGE
PRESS

Interior and Cover Designer: Lisa Schreiber
Art Manager: Sara Feinstein
Editor: Shannon Criss
Production Editor: Ashley Polikoff
Illustrations used under license from Creative Market/Statement Goods. Author photo courtesy of © Sofia Grady.

ISBN: Print 978-1-64739-184-3 | eBook 978-1-64739-185-0

R0

Contents

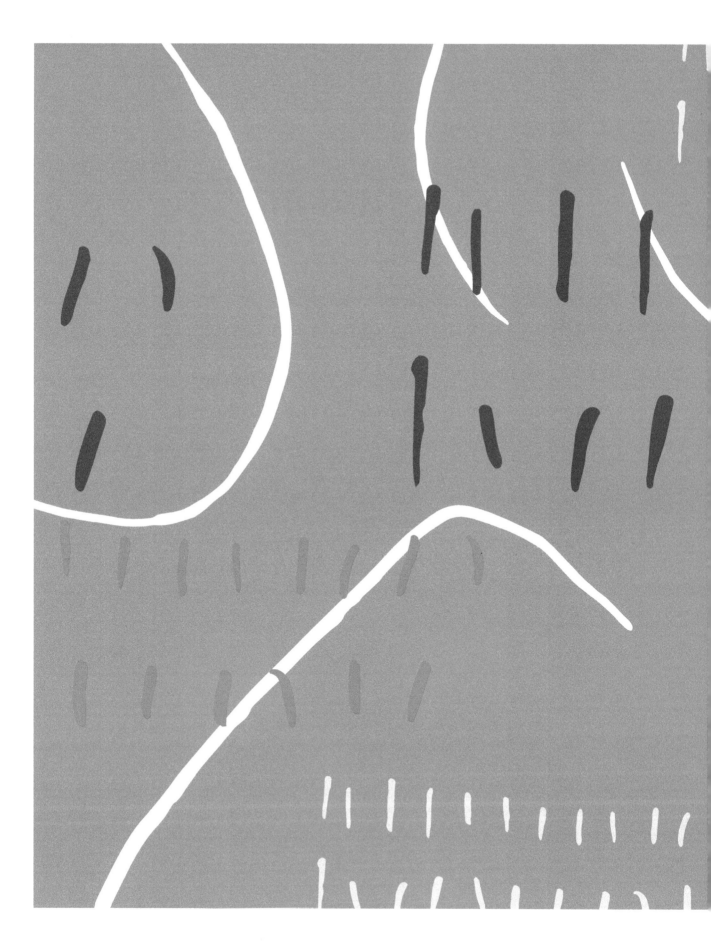

Introduction

According to the National Domestic Violence Hotline, almost half of all women and men in the United States have reported experiencing psychological abuse by an intimate partner in their lifetime (48.4% and 48.8%, respectively). Research conducted by Dr. Judy Blando at the University of Phoenix states that almost 75% of employees surveyed have been impacted by workplace bullying as both a witness and a target.

My name is Theresa Comito and I'm a licensed marriage and family therapist practicing in California. I have worked with victims and survivors of emotional abuse throughout my career, but exclusively for ten years. One of my earliest clients shared that a social worker had told her that if she did not leave her abusive partner and another incident was reported at her home, social services would take her children away from her. At the time, I'm sure this social worker thought she was providing my client with the motivation or "tough love" she needed to leave. But, instead, my client stopped sharing what was happening in her home and shut me and others out, even when the situation turned violent. The reasons victims stay in abusive relationships is complex. The tenacity and endurance of my clients, and my loved ones, reflect this complexity. I feel blessed to know so many resilient and outspoken survivors, and I'm honored that they have shared their stories with me. I recognize and understand the effort it takes to survive and to recover. But recover they did, as you can too.

The intent of this book is to help you acknowledge, understand, and recover from emotional abuse. If you are reading this book, it's likely because you know something is wrong. You may not know how to describe or define it but you are looking for answers and help with finding solutions. It's important to understand that healing will be a process, and you can't do it alone. Enlist the help and support of loved ones, friends, family members, and coworkers, if they are available to you. It is also important to seek support from professionals who understand what you are experiencing. Counselors, social workers, therapists, and support groups can all help while you rebuild or enhance your network of supporters. Search for a service provider online, contact your insurance company or your HR department, but actively seek support. It will be vital to your recovery.

This workbook will let you channel the complexities of abuse and recovery into tangible concepts and exercises. As you complete the exercises on these pages, you will uncover the patterns and dynamics of your relationships, identify your strengths and values, discover your resilience, and learn practical strategies to manage daily challenges and promote improved self-worth and sense of well-being.

HOW TO USE THIS BOOK

This workbook provides a private space for healing, just you and the page, where you can come to terms with what you have experienced. It can be an emotional process, and as you move through the work in this book, you may experience strong emotions. Be patient with yourself, take breaks when you need to, but don't give up.

Seek professional advice and support if you think you may be in any danger. Physical abuse is nearly always preceded and accompanied by emotional abuse. Risk is increased when trying to leave these relationships.

As healing is progressive, this book is progressive in its design. We begin by building a foundation of information so that you have the chance to address your experiences within the context of the collective. Then we move into a guided examination of your relationships where I will lead you through a series of exercises and self-assessments, and, ultimately, direct you on your path to building new and healthier skills. It is not intended for the work to be done hastily. Most of the exercises ask you to reflect, meaning these ideas should be considered carefully and contemplated over some time. If you have trusted friends, family, or a therapist, I would encourage sharing and discussing some of these ideas with those people in your life. It is best to work from the beginning to the end of the book because of the sequencing, and you will be encouraged throughout to refer back to content in part 1 as you progress through the book.

Recovery is the process of regaining possession or control of something that was stolen or lost.

Choosing a Therapist

If you feel that therapy might be helpful, sooner is better. Therapy can help increase your insight and self-awareness, help you clarify your goals, and support you while you are making difficult choices.

Look for a therapist who has experience working with victims of abuse. Speaking with a therapist who has experience with abuse and trauma can help you deal with the depression and anxiety that often follow an abusive relationship. A therapist can help you process the painful memories or experiences so that it is possible to move on. They can also aid you in learning to regulate your strong emotions.

The most important thing I can tell you about finding a therapist is to find one you like. Find one who makes you feel comfortable and understood. The relationship you have with your therapist is the most powerful healing factor. Call more than one prospective therapist, and ask any questions you may have. Ask friends, family members, and other professionals for recommendations. If it turns out that you are not comfortable with the therapist you have chosen, don't hesitate to change therapists.

Some additional things to keep in mind:

- It is typical to feel a little nervous when starting therapy.
- The first session or two will focus on information gathering.
- Therapy is collaborative; be as honest as you can with your therapist.
- Ask questions and express any concerns you have with the therapist, especially concerns about the therapy or their behavior.
- Make sure you have worked out the payment arrangements beforehand. Check insurance coverage or fees and how the therapist expects to be paid, including cancellation policies, and so on.

PART I

Identifying Emotional Abuse

PART 1 OF THIS BOOK is intended to help you recognize, acknowledge, and understand emotional abuse, as well as begin the process of recovery.

Emotional abuse is more difficult to identify than physical abuse, although physical abuse is almost always accompanied by emotional abuse. The invisible nature of emotional abuse, and a lack of understanding of precisely just what it is, makes this identification difficult. Emotional abuse can exist in the form of "playful" teasing, sarcasm, or jokes. It is frequently verbally aggressive and threatening, but does not often begin that way.

Emotional abuse is systematic, nonphysical bullying. It encompasses a pattern of behaviors used against the victim to hurt, undermine, and control them. The abuser's primary mission is control. As a victim of emotional abuse, you may experience anxiety, depression, low self-esteem, confusion, difficulty concentrating or making decisions, and other physical symptoms.

Healing from emotional abuse is possible. The first steps in your recovery will include identifying what happened to you, understanding that it is not your fault, and recognizing that nothing you did caused your abuser to act this way. Understanding the profile and tactics of the abuser can help clear up the confusion that resulted from the abuser's contradictory behavior and communication, and prepare you to act on your own behalf.

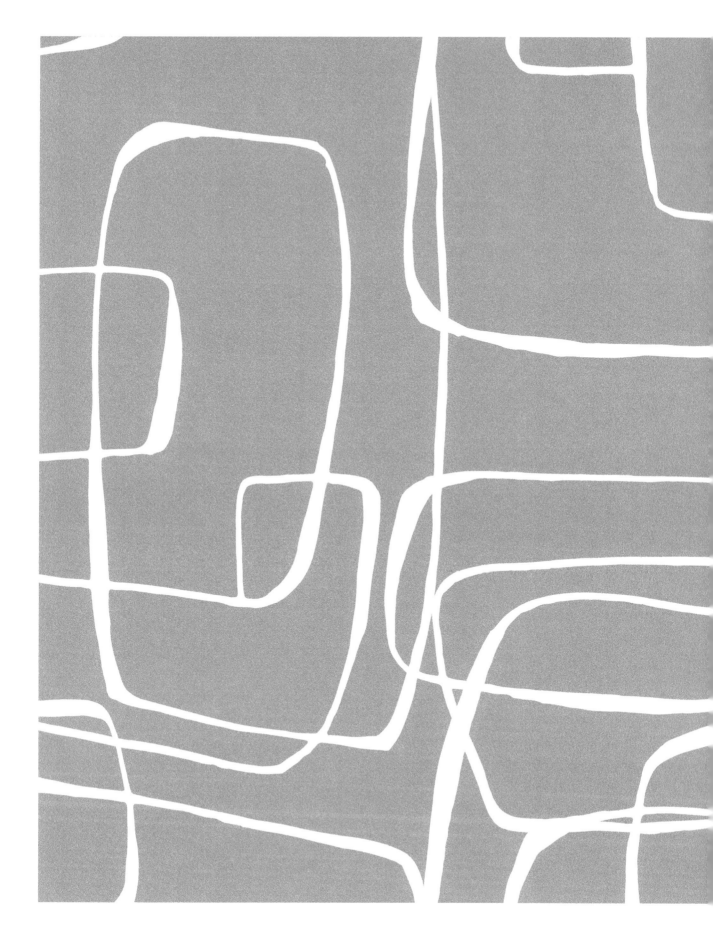

CHAPTER 1

Understanding Emotional Abuse

The impact of emotional abuse on a person is just as damaging as the effects of physical abuse, and often even more so. To illustrate this point, consider that in an incident of physical assault, the victim may have physical evidence, such as bruises. They may have the opportunity to take legal action through filing charges or seeking protection through a restraining order. However, that is not the case in emotional abuse incidents. Emotional abuse is a more pervasive form of abuse that, in most cases, precedes and accompanies physical and sexual abuse.

Emotional or psychological abuse can be a more effective means of control because it undermines the victim's self-confidence and makes them question their own perceptions. It can destroy you from the inside out. It is the two-step alternation between loving and abusive behaviors that makes it so effective.

Emotional abuse includes any nonphysical behavior—both overt and covert tactics—that occur as a pattern over time. These tactics include criticism (insults, name-calling, infantilization), hostility (yelling, silent treatment, verbal aggression), intimidation (posturing, threats), humiliation (using what they know about you to embarrass you), and harassment (persistent, repetitive demands). The intent is to control or dominate the victim, which can result in low self-worth, fear, mental health symptoms, and suicidal thoughts. Emotional and mental abuse are part of a larger overarching term—psychological violence. Psychological violence can be defined as behaviors and communication founded on control, disapproval, and domination. Power imbalances exist in these relationships, so abuse can be experienced in a variety of relationships, such as between intimate partners, parent and child, and supervisor and employee.

SIGNS OF EMOTIONAL ABUSE

Behaviors described in this section focus on power and control tactics. These behaviors are easier to understand when we view them on a continuum instead of as entirely good or bad. Intimate relationships rarely appear abusive at the start. In fact, early onset of abusive behaviors often appears attentive and nurturing. However, caretaking behavior can be a form of control.

Learning about your new partner can be fun and exciting at the beginning of a relationship. Sometimes, though, you can have a feeling or a reaction to something your new partner says or does that doesn't feel right. You may experience a sinking feeling in your gut, warning signs we refer to as "red flags." Sometimes we can get caught up in the novelty or excitement of a new relationship and want to ignore these signs, but pay close attention to your gut feelings. Take the time to carefully examine your partner's words, actions, and intentions. It is important to recognize these signs so you can act as soon as possible.

CONTROL

Control is a primary concept in understanding abuse. All tactics or signs of abuse described in this chapter relate to the abuser maintaining control over you. It may come at first in the form of attentiveness, protection, and nurturing. However, in an abusive relationship, these behaviors are an attempt to manage aspects of your life. It is common for an abusive partner to keep track of where you go and where you are, insist on being in constant contact with you, tell you who you can and cannot see, what you should wear, and so on. The abuser may be demanding and angry, or may offer more gentle "helpful suggestions." They may embed criticism in these demands, or you may notice over time that when you don't take their suggestions, there are consequences.

NAME-CALLING

Name-calling, or verbal insults designed to win an argument, demean, or control your feelings of self-worth, can be overt or disguised by joking or playfulness. The intent is always to belittle and devalue the victim. When arguments consistently devolve into assassinating your character and include "always" and "never" statements, they serve no purpose other than to control, undermine, and dominate you.

An example of this is, "You always forget to do what I asked you. Are you just dumb or is there something else wrong with you?"

YELLING

Yelling is commonly known as the raising of someone's voice, but abusers use yelling as a form of conditioning. The receiver is conditioned to be compliant with the yeller, who attempts to impose their will with this behavior. Yelling is a way of wearing down the victim and preventing their expression. Over time, it can whittle away a person's spirit and dignity.

GASLIGHTING

Gaslighting—a common topic in recent years—is a term taken from a stage play called *Gas Light* from the 1930s, where a husband plotted his wife's demise by manipulating her into thinking she was crazy. Gaslighting strategies include when the abuser

- withholds information
- puts their spin on information to fit their agenda
- uses jokes and sarcasm to dismiss the victim's feelings and experiences
- denies and minimizes a victim's reactions and concerns
- acts as though they or the victim did not say what they said or that certain events did not actually happen

Gaslighting can cause an abuse victim to doubt their own perceptions and sense of reality. Common gaslighting phrases may look like the following:

- "I never said that."
- "You never told me that."
- "That never happened."
- "Are you sure you didn't dream that?"
- "You're too sensitive."

Abusers who engage in gaslighting tactics often project onto you things that they have done, such as telling you that you're confused, crazy, or intoxicated if you say what you know to be true or question their version of the facts. In a work environment, the abuser may take credit for your work or ideas and then deny it. They may lie to others about you, or take a sliver of truth and blow it up in a way that ruins your reputation. Gaslighters attack you with information they know to be especially important or sensitive.

ISOLATION

An abusive person perceives your spending time with friends and family as a threat and can work to isolate you from them. They may begin this process by criticizing or devaluing your relationships with your friends and family. For example, the abuser may say that your loved ones treat you poorly or take advantage of you, or that time spent with them takes away from your relationship with the abuser.

There may be enough truth in this coercion to influence or confuse you. For instance, you may have confided in your partner at some point about frustrations with a family member, and your partner will remind you of this when you are planning on spending time with that person. Attempts to isolate you are sometimes much more overt. Your abuser may restrict your access to money, transportation, or communication with your friends and family. The loneliness that results from this social isolation can lead to anxiety, depression, increased substance use, and health issues.

THREATS

A threat is a statement of intent to cause you damage, pain, or loss. It is an act of coercion from an abuser, with an undercurrent of the potential for violence.

The fear of what could happen to you becomes a powerful motivator for you to try to manage the relationship and accommodate the abuser. These or similar statements—all reported by victims of abuse—will often target a fear you already have:

- "I will kill myself."
- "I will kill you."
- "If I can't have you, no one will."
- "I will take the kids."
- "I will turn you in to immigration."
- "I will out you to your family."

- "I will ruin your life."
- "I will leave you without a dime."
- "I'm going to sleep with other people."
- "I will never let you go."
- "Maybe you just don't want to work here anymore."

PUNISHMENT

Punishment is anything your abuser may do in response to any injury, refusal, or perceived rejection. Punishment can come in the form of revenge or conditioning. An abuser seeks revenge to inflict pain and conditions you in an attempt to change your behavior.

REJECTING

Rejecting behavior is any act that refuses to acknowledge your needs and gifts. It can include withdrawing or declining offers of love, attention, or affection. It is a way of denigrating you and what you have to offer, with the underlying message that you're not wanted or needed.

NEGLECT

Neglect is a pattern of behaviors used to remove attention and affection, and to deprive you of your emotional need for belonging, love, and connection. Neglect includes careless behaviors, ignoring, showing interest in other partners, and the silent treatment.

FINANCIAL ABUSE

Financial abuse includes limiting access to funds, withholding financial information, or imposing absolute control of funds—often resembling a parent-to-child dynamic. It is not uncommon in this type of abuse for the victim to have no idea how much their partner makes or to be required to turn over their whole paycheck to the abuser.

Signs of a Healthy Relationship

While no relationship is perfect, a healthy relationship is characterized by respect and trust. Each relationship is unique, but healthy relationships share common factors, such as those included below:

- We listen to each other.
- We take each other's concerns seriously.
- We are each responsible for our own actions.
- We are supportive of the other trying new things.
- We can argue and still feel loved.
- We trust one another.
- We share our past.
- We express appreciation for each other.
- We greet each other when coming and going.
- We make decisions together.
- We respect each other's boundaries. We can accept no as an answer.
- We are affectionate and playful.
- We value and respect each other's relationships with friends and family.
- When stressed or upset, we turn to each other for understanding and support.
- We encourage growth in each other.
- We allow for and learn from our mistakes.

PHYSICAL SIDE EFFECTS OF EMOTIONAL ABUSE

Emotional abuse can cause several long-term effects for the victim. As individuals try to cope with the emotional effects of abuse, they may also start to experience some physiological effects. It may be difficult for victims to connect their experience of abuse to their physical symptoms. The victim's feelings of confusion, shame, and fear can further contribute to the difficulty in identifying these physical effects.

ANXIETY

Are you currently or have you experienced the following symptoms of anxiety?

☐ fatigue	☐ shortness of breath
☐ headaches	☐ dizziness
☐ muscle tension	☐ abdominal distress
☐ aches and pains	☐ feeling flushed or chilled
☐ trembling	☐ tingling or numb hands
☐ twitching	☐ memory problems
☐ sweating	☐ inability to concentrate
☐ chest pain	☐ racing thoughts
☐ heart palpitations	☐ agitation

CHRONIC PAIN

We know there is a connection between abuse and trauma and chronic pain. While the reasons aren't completely clear, it is believed that the chronic stress we experience in an abusive relationship causes overactivation of the fight-or-flight response. This natural response releases stress hormones and suppresses our immune system. Overactivation of these stress hormones impairs the regulation of immune system functioning and produces increased inflammation in our systems. This can put us at risk for health conditions and chronic pain.

GUILT

Targets of emotional abuse may find themselves vulnerable to guilt. An emotionally abusive partner may blame you for any problems they experience, including the abuse they inflict on you. The physical effects of guilt can include insomnia, a loss of appetite, sadness, and regret. Guilt can feel a lot like depression, and clinical depression can result from ongoing feelings of guilt and a false sense of responsibility to an abusive partner.

INSOMNIA

Many people who are emotionally abused have difficulty falling asleep or staying asleep. Chronic stress and emotional abuse can lead to increased arousal—the body's response to a chronic threat. This results in muscle tension and an inability to relax, which can make it difficult to sleep. Sleep deprivation can have long-term effects, both physically and mentally. Attention to self-care and sleep hygiene are vital to our recovery.

SOCIAL WITHDRAWAL

Social withdrawal may result from the frequent insults to our self-esteem, which can cause feelings of shame, among other physical and emotional symptoms. Ongoing emotional abuse wears us down and makes us much more likely to isolate ourselves from friends and family. This cuts us off from the opinions of others, and from the emotional support our friends and family provide. Our loved ones don't have access to us and can't notice the effects the abuse has on us.

Journaling Exercise

Take some time to reflect on the effect that emotional abuse has taken on your body. Begin by doing this simple body scan, an exercise that will guide you to turn your attention to each part of your body and notice where you are holding tension.

Get into a comfortable position, and beginning with your toes, scan up through your whole body. Proceed slowly, calling attention to each body part, inside and out. Focus on your breathing, pushing your belly out on the inhale and pulling it in on the exhale.

> After completing the first scan of your body, repeat it, but this time notice and write about each part where you find tension or pain. Consider how your tension or pain is affected or stimulated by the abuse you are experiencing or have experienced.

_____

_____

_____

_____

_____

_____

_____

_____

UNDERSTANDING EMOTIONAL ABUSE

"Why?" or "Why me?"
"What is it about me that attracts this type of person?"
"I am a magnet for abusive people."

I have heard people in emotionally abusive relationships ask these questions repeatedly.

My experience has taught me that there is a common thread among victims of abusive relationships. Working with my clients has made it clear that each person entered these relationships with a vulnerability of some kind. Vulnerability, in this context, refers to:

- a difficult life event around the time you met your abuser
- a history of childhood abuse

- dysfunctional family of origin dynamics
- addiction or substance abuse
- disability
- membership in a marginalized group, such as race, immigration status, gender, gender identity, sexual orientation
- personal qualities, for example, empathic, sensitive, compassionate

The following stories are several case examples:

A Cancer Survivor

After recovering from cancer treatments, a woman felt unattractive due to hair and weight loss, and lucky to have a "second chance" at life. She then met a man who was "protective" of her, didn't take no for an answer because he said he knew what was best for her, and showered her with attention and promises of a bright future and children. As the relationship progressed, the behaviors that originally appeared as signs of his love and connection amplified. Protection turned into control of her movements. He disrespected her boundaries—she wasn't allowed to say no, and he made all the decisions. He began to limit her contact with friends and family, saying, "They don't care for you the way I do." After the birth of their children, the gaslighting began: "You are ungrateful for the life I gave back to you."

An Accomplished Nurse

A nurse close to retirement had been working at her job for 26 years, when a new manager arrived. The abuse began almost from day one, with the manager finding small details to criticize, frequently in public; changing policies and procedures without notification; and choosing night shifts to burst in and yell at her when she was working alone. In her sixties, fearing loss of her pension, and doubting her ability to find another job, she tried to cope with the bullying until she began having panic attacks.

A Childhood Abuse Survivor

A young man who was physically abused by his father throughout his childhood became involved with a young woman whom he described later as having a "Jekyll and Hyde" personality. He describes his response to her yells, threats, and constant criticism:

"When she gets angry, her voice changes and somehow I feel like a child again. I feel the way I did when my father was angry and I knew a beating was coming. I get quiet and scared. It seems bizarre because I am twice her size, but I don't feel like I can do anything else. I am a man, so I can't tell anyone. They'll think I'm weak. How can I leave her? I am responsible for her."

Honoring Her Father

A woman I worked with met a young man through her father. Her father mentored this young man because he had a difficult and abusive upbringing. The woman felt immediately uncomfortable around the young man. Her father was diagnosed with a terminal illness and died within a year. While he was ill, the woman began dating the young man because it seemed to please her father and rushed into marriage so her father could attend their wedding. After her father's death, her husband began taking over aspects of her life and her business "to help her." As she emerged from her grief and began to come back to her life, his criticism and efforts to isolate her became increasingly aggressive.

Undocumented and Vulnerable

I worked with a woman who came to the United States from her home country to escape the difficult conditions and lack of opportunities for her children there. As an undocumented woman with children, her options for work were limited and exploitive. She met a "charming man, who was attentive and very generous" with both her and her kids. After she was hooked and began living with him, he controlled everything she did and threatened to turn her in to the immigration authorities if she did not obey his directives.

PROFILE OF THE ABUSER

Many people in abusive relationships wonder if there were warning signs they should have seen but did not recognize at first. Abusive relationships frequently begin with quick involvement, overattentiveness, preoccupation with the victim's safety or well-being, and unrealistic expectations about the relationship. The following are all well-known signs of an emotional abuser.

TAKES NO RESPONSIBILITY

The abuser will not admit fault or take responsibility for their behavior. If they have difficulty at work or cannot hold a job, it is because they are treated unfairly. If they engage in abusive behavior toward someone else, it is the victim's fault for making them angry. Maybe it is the abuser's terrible upbringing or the drinking that made them act out. No matter what happens, or how obvious their role in the situation, it's not their fault. In fact, it's often your fault or someone else's. Every apology is accompanied by a qualifying statement, like "If you just hadn't done that, it never would have happened."

VOID OF EMOTION/LACKS EMOTIONAL SELF-CONTROL

The abusive person may vacillate between a complete lack of emotional control and a cold and distant response to your emotional pain. The hallmark of the healthy personality is flexibility and the ability to regulate emotions. An individual with an abusive personality may overregulate their emotions, which might appear as numbness. If they underregulate their emotions, they may be reactive, irritable, or angry. Victims may experience their partner/abuser as a "Dr. Jekyll and Mr. Hyde" type. The abuser's dramatic mood swings and hypersensitivity often make victims feel confused and on edge. The abusive personality is fragile—easily insulted or offended, and often defensive.

JEALOUS DEVICES

Jealousy is often discussed and justified by an abuser in terms of its relationship to love: "I am jealous because I love you so much." Jealousy, however, has nothing to do with love. Instead, it indicates possessiveness, control, and a lack of trust. Jealous behaviors include questioning a partner's whereabouts or intentions, and misreading facts to justify controlling behaviors.

The abuser may do the following:

- question what you wear
- question who you are dressing for
- check your phone messages
- check the mileage on your car
- call or text frequently
- expect an immediate response to any communication
- use anything less than an immediate response to justify their jealousy and prove you are lying

PLAYS THE VICTIM

Abusers respond to typical setbacks as though they are being personally attacked and targeted, and when confronted, they rewrite history. They portray themselves as self-sacrificing and you as ungrateful, perhaps accounting all the ways you benefit and they suffer. Ultimately, you end up feeling like you have not been a good enough partner, child, friend, or employee.

VANITY

A vain person is preoccupied with their image, accomplishments, appearance, and qualities. An abusive partner may frequently tell their partner about all the abuser's good qualities and actions, and how lucky the victim is to have them. The abuser may use that image to control the other person's behavior, threatening to leave them if they make the abuser look bad.

PERSONALITY DISORDERS OF THE ABUSER

A personality disorder is a pattern of experience and behavior that deviates from the cultural norm, and causes marked distress and impairment in functioning. It's an inflexible pattern, pervasive across a range of settings and relationships, that affects the way a person thinks and perceives the world, themselves, and others. Their emotions and ability to manage them, their relationship skills, and their ability to control their impulses are consistently problematic. It is important to clarify that not everyone who is abusive in their relationships suffers from a personality disorder or mental illness. The following descriptions are based on the criteria for each diagnosis in the *Diagnostic and Statistical Manual of Mental Disorders, Fifth Edition.*

ANTISOCIAL PERSONALITY DISORDER (APD)

An individual with APD doesn't respect laws or societal norms. They are deceitful, impulsive, aggressive, and irritable. They exhibit a disregard for safety, are irresponsible, and lack remorse for their behaviors. They consistently violate the rights of others. In relationships they are manipulative to gain power or profit.

NARCISSISTIC PERSONALITY DISORDER (NPD)

The word *narcissist* and the acronym NPD have come into common usage in recent years. In the clinical sense, a person with NPD has a grandiose sense of self-importance, has a sense of entitlement, requires admiration, believes they are superior to others, and demonstrates a lack of empathy. The person with NPD exploits their relationships for personal gain, feels envious of others or believes others are envious of them, and behaves in arrogant ways. They want to associate only with others they perceive as being of the same high status as themselves, but will devalue anyone who disappoints them. Individuals with NPD are highly sensitive to insults or injury to their self-esteem. Rage and counterattacks are the most likely responses to perceived insults.

BORDERLINE PERSONALITY DISORDER (BPD)

The individual with BPD is characterized by their intense fear of abandonment, unstable identity, and intense interpersonal relationships. They are impulsive, and it is typical for people with BPD to display recurrent suicidal behavior or threats of self-harm, mood instability, reactivity, anger, or stress-related paranoia. In relationships, they tend to alternate between idealizing and devaluing their partners.

HISTRIONIC PERSONALITY DISORDER (HPD)

An individual with HPD exhibits a pattern of excessive emotionality and attention-seeking behaviors. The person with HPD needs to be the center of attention, and achieves that through displays of rapidly changing emotion, sexual or provocative behaviors, and use of physical appearance to draw attention to themselves. They are easily influenced by others and consider their relationships more intimate than they are. In relationships, they tend to be dependent and are manipulative to gain nurturing.

GOALS OF THE EMOTIONAL ABUSER

The emotional abuser's goal is to maintain control of their victim. The abuser wants the final word in every decision, to gain and maintain the upper hand. The abuser manipulates your thoughts and emotions by undermining your confidence, diminishing your self-esteem, and making you doubt your own judgment and sanity. The emotional abuser wants to dominate you, and the most effective way to do this is to create the right conditions to weaken your sense of self-efficacy or belief in your ability to handle situations in your life. The following list highlights the methods abusers use to dominate victims.

CONTROL

Control is both a tool and a goal for the abuser. The goal is to control every aspect of your life, because you are only there to meet the abuser's needs. Control serves to undermine your self-efficacy. The abuser promotes their grandiose sense of self, boosting their sense of importance and superiority through controlling another. Insecurity, stress relief, and fear of abandonment are all possible reasons one person seeks to dominate another.

BELITTLE

The goal of belittling is to make you feel less than you are. An abusive person in your life may choose to criticize things that you feel good about or proud of, and either directly or indirectly diminish your accomplishments and you in the process. Criticism can include belittling, making you the butt of jokes in front of others, or disregarding or ignoring your feelings and opinions. An abuser may remind you of past mistakes and failures, and then accuse you of being oversensitive and overreacting.

A client reported that she did all the housework, shopping, and cooking for her emotionally abusive partner. Every time she started to prepare his meals after her workday—when she arrived home at least two hours after him—he began his commentary and frequently joked with their friends about what a terrible cook she was:

- "What are you putting in that?"
- "That smells terrible."
- "You can barely boil water."

DEVALUE

Devaluing is a device frequently employed by abusers, who will choose a strength, talent, or something they previously liked about you as the subject. It is a common and much-written-about aspect of the narcissistic abuser's tactic. This tactic paired with its opposite—idealizing—is a powerful combination. In my practice, I refer to this as the abuser's ability to speak out of both sides of their mouth. The victim often feels dejected by the devaluing statement and feels a powerful pull to reinstate themselves with the abuser, regaining approval and idealization.

SHAME

It is important to make a distinction between guilt and shame. Guilt says, "I made a mistake," while shame says, "You are a mistake." The abuser's shame-inducing global statements typically insult your worth, your abilities, and who you are as a person. The abuser will choose criticisms of things they know are sensitive topics to induce shame:

- "You never get it right."
- "You always let me down."
- "You can't do anything right."

CHAPTER WRAP-UP

This chapter is the foundation for the rest of the book. It provided you with information to increase your understanding and awareness of emotional abuse. The more information you have about what happened to you and how you have been impacted, the better equipped you will be to move on from the effects of emotional abuse. Knowledge is power.

The chapter also deconstructed abuse into its component parts:

- signs
- abusive tactics
- context (power and control)

These components employed by the abuser provide insight and clarification that you are not to blame for being on the receiving end of abusive behavior.

Descriptions of the abusive personality highlight the abuser's motivation and amplify the fact that their actions serve their own needs. Educating yourself brings validation and clarity to all you have experienced. Return to this chapter as you complete the exercises in this book if you find yourself feeling confused or if you experience self-doubt.

CHAPTER 2

Grief

We often experience grief in response to loss. Grief that is experienced post-abuse is complicated and confusing. If you have removed yourself from the relationship with an abusive boss, family member, or partner, you are likely cycling through a lot of contradictory feelings. You are likely angry and sad and would rather not feel this way. It is important to give yourself time and space to grieve. We may experience grief as sorrow or as pining. When we express sorrow, we are feeling the absence of that person in our life. When we pine, we wish for things to return to the way they were before. Resist the urge to pine for how it used to be, as it will not move you forward in your grieving process. It is more than likely that the relationship was never as you initially perceived it anyway.

HOW DID YOU SURVIVE YOUR RELATIONSHIP?

As an abusive relationship progresses, we are gradually altered. As life becomes more difficult and confusing, we adapt to the abuse in ways that make it easier to function in our daily lives and prevent us from feeling helpless and out of control. While we needed these adaptations to keep us afloat, the victim's coping skills consequently serve to justify, minimize, and excuse the abuser's behavior. The same defenses that helped us survive may have contributed to our staying trapped in the relationship. When dealing with regret and self-blame, take the time to acknowledge your resilience in surviving the abuse.

The grief experienced after the end of an abusive relationship can be more complicated, and you may find yourself wondering what you are grieving. If the relationship was bad, what do you have to grieve? It's important to note that we can still suffer losses, even when we decide to leave an abusive relationship. Some losses that can occur are:

- relationships/community—friends or family connected to the abusive person
- material things
- lifestyle
- sense of safety
- sense of self
- worldview or faith
- pets

Many of us have been exposed to the stages of grief first developed by Elisabeth Kübler-Ross during her work with terminally ill patients. The stages of denial, anger, bargaining, depression, and acceptance are common reactions to loss, but we often don't experience them in a linear way. We may also experience some, but not all, of these stages, or we may experience them in a random order. These feelings may also arise in response to triggers that remind us of our loss—including time of year, milestone dates like a birthday or anniversary, or the sight of others in healthy relationships when we have lost ours. We may also experience shock, yearning, loneliness, disorganized thoughts, and mixed or contradictory emotions. Feelings of lost time are also common following the loss of an abusive relationship.

A client contemplating ending her relationship said, "I have been with this person for seven years, and for seven years I have struggled and fought for the relationship. I lost family and friends for the relationship. If I let it go now, what does that say about the last seven years? It feels like a devastating loss that I may not ever recover from."

You may experience feeling misunderstood and unsupported when trying to deal with this grief. Friends and family may not respond the way you hoped. They may say that it was a terrible relationship ("So what is there to grieve?") or that you should be happy and relieved, and just ready to move on.

Know that the last thing you need is to feel bad for already feeling bad. You are grieving the loss of your relationship and the intangible things that have been taken from you. This may include your prior self-image, aspects of your identity, self-respect, optimism, sense of safety, and faith. Understanding and acknowledging the abuse in your relationship is a powerful, life-changing experience, but it hurts! With this knowledge, memories are altered, and regret and anger can loom large for some time.

As a frequent catalyst for change, anger can be an extremely important stage in the recovery process. It allows us to set a boundary and provides the energy we need to begin the recovery process. The following exercises are designed to help you explore and move through your grief and loss.

Hopes and Dreams

We all enter relationships with some fantasies about what they will bring to our lives and our future, so a part of what we grieve when they end is the hopes and dreams we had for the relationship. You will need some time to do this exercise, and it is recommended that you be as specific as possible. Find a comfortable and quiet place to sit, and begin by remembering. Float back to a very early time in your relationship. Now begin to reflect on what you imagined the relationship would bring to your life. Write about those fantasies in as much detail as possible.

_____

_____

_____

_____

_____

_____

_____

_____

_____

_____

Speaking Back to the Fantasy

Now we will compare fantasy versus reality. Look at your hopes and dreams from the previous exercise, and create a shorthand title or nickname for the hopes and dreams you had for the relationship. List hopes down the left side of the page. Now revisit the top of the list and write down what actually happened in the relationship. For example, "I thought we would explore our creativity together" versus "The abuser was competitive and demeaning."

HOPES AND DREAMS	ACTUAL EVENTS

HOPES AND DREAMS	ACTUAL EVENTS

Exploring Cultural Myths of Romantic Love

Read the following statements that reflect cultural myths about love. Place a check mark next to each statement that may have influenced your thoughts about staying in your relationship at some point.

- ☐ Love is enough to make the relationship work.
- ☐ Having an instant attraction and sexual chemistry is "true love."
- ☐ We all have a soul mate out there, one true love.
- ☐ You can be sarcastic and competitive with each other while falling in love.
- ☐ Jealousy just means my partner really loves me.
- ☐ There is a high level of conflict in the relationship because there is so much passion in the relationship.
- ☐ Violence and abuse are hot.
- ☐ Stalking is flattering and romantic.
- ☐ My partner always has my best interests at heart, and their feedback is just "tough love" that is meant to help me.
- ☐ You can treat people poorly, say you're sorry, and they will still love you.

Myths about Love

How did these myths about love interfere with your feelings and choices about the relationship when trouble began? Write about at least two instances where you were influenced by one or more of these myths.

1. _____

_____

_____

_____

_____

_____

_____

_____

2. _____

_____

_____

_____

_____

_____

_____

_____

Exploring Myths about Fairness

Read the following list and checkmark each item that influenced a decision you made regarding the abuse you were subjected to.

☐ We live in a meritocracy—a system where people achieve and move up in the system based upon their achievements and efforts.

☐ What goes around comes around. The abuser will get what's coming to them.

☐ If I focus and do everything right, I will be rewarded.

☐ Those in power are right, because they hold power, and they value fairness and justice.

☐ Objectivity and truth govern our societal and workplace norms.

☐ If I experience difficulty or conflict in a relationship, it is because I am doing something wrong, or I must deserve this treatment.

Assumptions about Fairness

Reflect on your own sense of fairness and how that influences your assumptions about others. Set a timer for five minutes and write your thoughts and feelings about this concept. Just keep your hand moving to block the inner critic—the voice inside you that tells you what you are thinking and writing are wrong.

_____

_____

_____

_____

_____

_____

_____

_____

_____

_____

Long-held beliefs from childhood or religious values, in addition to messages we received about ourselves from the abuser, can interfere with or influence our interpretation of events as they occur. We may know in our head that something is not true, yet still operate from underlying beliefs adopted in childhood that lie just beneath our awareness. In fact, some of the power an abuser wields over us may be rooted in our irrational or distorted underlying beliefs—some we brought with us to the relationship, and some given to us by the abusive person in our life via the tactics explored in chapter 1.

Exploring Myths about Abuse

Now let's explore some myths about abuse. Checkmark the box next to each underlying belief that has influenced your feelings about yourself and contributed to your denial or minimization of the abuse.

☐ If someone is angry with me, it's because I did something to cause it.

☐ Family members love each other and only want to help.

☐ This is a professional environment. If the behavior was abusive, this supervisor couldn't get away with it.

- [ ] My partner is a religious person and would never abuse me, as it is against their values.

- [ ] My supervisor is highly regarded because they hold a position of authority. I must be doing something to provoke this behavior.

- [ ] It's just their sense of humor. They meant to be funny, not to harm me.

- [ ] I am not able to receive feedback.

- [ ] I am overly sensitive.

- [ ] I can fix this person.

- [ ] If I change my behavior, the abuse will stop.

- [ ] A woman can't abuse a man.

- [ ] My partner doesn't mean to hurt me; they just got angry.

Debunking myths will allow us to clearly identify what has been lost and to fully grieve our losses.

Exploring Underlying Beliefs

How did myths or underlying beliefs undermine your efforts to act on your own behalf or serve to keep you in a cycle of self-blame and shame?

_____

_____

_____

_____

_____

Exploring the Ripple Effects of the Abusive Relationship

Using the following circles, we will explore the losses you experienced due to the abuse. Go back to the list of things lost in the beginning of this chapter (see page 22).

In the center circle, write something that you lost due to the abusive relationship. Then label the outer circles, as needed, with additional, more specific losses. For example, you may label the first circle "Relationships," then specify what relationships were lost or damaged by the abuse in additional circles. Use the lines that follow to reflect on this exercise.

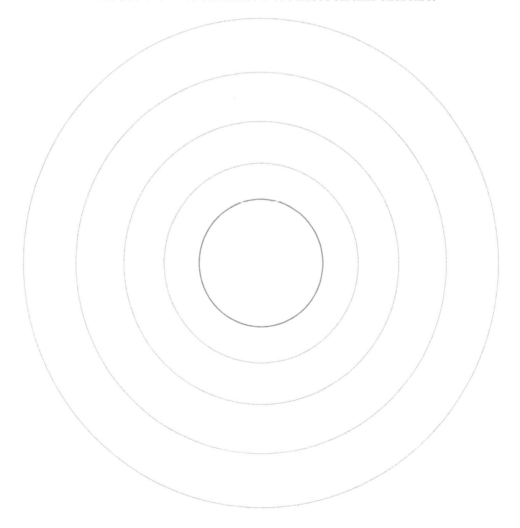

_____

_____

_____

_____

Creating a Grief Journal

Journaling as a regular practice is a great addition to a self-care routine. Obtain a journal or make your own for this activity. A grief journal can be used to explore the depth and breadth of your grief, as well as to provide a time and place for you to express and manage your emotions. You can also use it to track your progress and increase your awareness of what triggers your grief.

On each page of the journal, you will include the following:

- date of the entry
- scale of your distress from 1 to 10 (1 being no distress, and 10 being intense distress)
- what prompted this entry
- ten-minute free-write, exploring the thoughts, feelings, and reactions to the loss you are currently experiencing

Here is an example of what your page might look like:

Date: January 20, 2020

Scale: 7/10

I am writing today because after spending time with my sister and her partner I felt sad.

I feel like I will always be alone, that I will never find another part-ner or be happy with anyone again. I felt jealous of their relationship even though I love them both and I'm happy they are together. Then I feel guilty for feeling jealous because they are so supportive of me.

Creating Rituals for Grieving

Rituals can be a powerful healing tool for managing grief. They can be used to remember or to release strong emotions. They can bring peace of clarity or assist you in feeling more grounded. Your reactions to these rituals may look very different from the grief you might experience at the death of a loved one, because you will likely want to reclaim some of what you are grieving.

Try the following rituals and make them your own:

- Allow yourself time to cry or feel. Use a timer, a candle, or some incense to set a clear amount of time for releasing emotion through tears.
- Choose a song, quote, or prayer that acknowledges your suffering and highlights that healing is possible. Perhaps you'll want to write it in your journal. A favorite quote of mine is from Albert Camus: "In the midst of winter, I found there was, within me, an invincible summer."
- Engage in an activity or experience that was prohibited in your relationship, something the abuser did not like you to do, eat, wear, or speak about. Fully acknowledge the feelings attached to this activity—the anxiety, fear, or guilt you may experience from doing it even now. Then create a motto for yourself about it, such as "From here on, I only need to please myself."
- Write out the negative labels your abuser used to devalue and belittle you. Now rip the paper into as many smaller pieces as possible, and discard them in the most satisfying way. Throw them in the trash, burn them in the fireplace, boil them in a pot of water, or flush them down the toilet. This ritual can be helpful in releasing some of your anger.
- Explore your emotions using a musical instrument or art materials, whichever feels more natural for you. Focus this exercise on the emotion attached to a particularly difficult memory or fact. For example, find a comfortable and private place to sit down and reflect on the painful memory. Be mindful of the sensations and feelings that come up when thinking of it. Now create a rhythm in music or visual art that accurately reflects the feeling.
- Create a visual representation of your grief, using pencils, markers, paints, or sculpting materials. You may notice that the messier the materials, the messier your emotions might feel, and that is okay.

Powerful Letter

Write a letter to the person who abused you that you do not send. Use the following structure to move through this process.

Dear _____,

When we met I thought _____

_____

_____

_____

_____

I believed that _____

_____

_____

_____

_____

And I felt _____

_____

_____

_____

_____

Then that first time you _____

_____

_____

*I felt*_____

_____

_____

but I thought _____

_____

_____

_____

_____

But now I know _____

_____

_____

_____

_____

I am letting you go now because _____

_____

_____

_____

_____

Be sure you give yourself enough time and space to complete each of these activities, and give yourself time for recovery afterward. A nourishing meal, a hot bath, or loving connection with friends or family will give you the opportunity to regulate your emotions.

CHAPTER WRAP-UP

In this chapter, we turned our focus to the complicated grief that arises when a person surfaces from an abusive relationship. It is not just the relationship that is lost; there is a myriad of associated wreckage. It is worthwhile to take the time and make the effort to examine the tangible losses as well as the intangible (the loss of a sense of safety and fairness, the loss of our hopes and dreams, and the ripple effects of the abuse), but it is painful. Consider how the view of yourself has been changed or lost. In this chapter, you also had the opportunity to explore previously held myths and beliefs about love, fairness, and abuse. While it may feel like you've had the rug pulled from underneath you, the deconstruction of these myths allows for the possibility of replacing old distorted assumptions with more advantageous ones.

CHAPTER 3

Acknowledgment and Awareness

I n previous chapters we have discussed what emotional abuse looks like, the profiles of the abusive person, and the impact abuse can have on the victim. In this chapter's exercises and activities, we explore your experiences in your intimate, work, or family relationships.

Without this understanding and acknowledgment of abuse there can be no movement forward toward recovery. It is important to understand that this process can be painful and distressing. You should take your time working through this section, and give yourself the time and space you need to regulate your emotions. Start by choosing a time and place that provides you with enough privacy and recovery time. During your recovery time, include soothing, pleasant, and nourishing activities or relaxation. A healthy meal, a hot bath, a cup of tea, or time engaging in your favorite hobby can help you feel restored.

Identifying Tactics of Your Abuser

What tactics has the abusive person in your life engaged in? Review the lists in chapter 1 (see pages 5 and 15), and fill in the following questions.

Write all the tactics you have experienced at the hands of your abuser.

_____

_____

_____

_____

_____

_____

_____

_____

Choose three of the most common tactics employed by your abuser. Write a brief example of each in the left-hand column, and the outcome on the right.

Here's an example:

Behavior = Criticized my clothing   Outcome = Changed my clothes

Behavior   Outcome

1. _____   1. _____

2. _____   2. _____

3. _____   3. _____

Reactions and Reflections:

_____

_____

_____

_____

_____

Previous Month Events

Place an X or X's on each day that you were the target of an abusive incident, conversation, or remark.

SUN	MON	TUES	WEDS	THURS	FRI	SAT

Write a narrative of the last abusive incident you can remember.

_____

_____

_____

_____

_____

_____

_____

_____

_____

_____

_____

_____

_____

Now review and reflect on the previous four exercises. You have just constructed a profile of the abusive relationship you have been subjected to. You may have a clearer picture of the types and frequency of the abusive behaviors and your responses and reactions to them.

Write a summary of the profile you constructed of your relationship— what your abuser did, how you became conditioned to respond, and the pattern and frequency of abuse.

_____

_____

_____

_____

_____

_____

_____

_____

_____

_____

Reread what you wrote in the previous section. Now imagine a beloved friend or family member was telling you that story.

Does it change how you feel about what happened? Why or why not?

_____

_____

_____

_____

_____

What would you say to them?

_____

_____

_____

_____

_____

Now go back to the time before this abusive person was in your life. Refer to the section *Understanding Emotional Abuse* (see page 11) in chapter 1 before proceeding.

What was happening then? Were you employed? Were you healthy? Were you in another relationship or just ending a relationship?

_____

_____

_____

_____

_____

What did your support system look like? Had you experienced a recent move or relocation? Had you experienced a recent loss? Were you using drugs or alcohol at that time? Do you belong to a group who is marginalized?

_____

_____

_____

_____

_____

Answer the questions as though you were telling someone a story about your life before the abuse occurred. You may choose to ask trusted friends and family to assist you in remembering as much as you can about that time.

_____

_____

_____

_____

_____

_____

_____

_____

_____

Take some time now to think about how others see you and how you see yourself. Draw a literal or abstract visual representation in each of the boxes. If you are more comfortable using words, proceed in that way.

How does your family of origin see you?	How do your friends see you?
How does the abuser see you?	How do you see yourself?

What did you learn from this exercise?

_____

_____

_____

_____

Using what you learned from this exercise, make a list of your best qualities.

_____

_____

_____

_____

_____

_____

_____

Exploring Your Family History

On the following page, create a diagram of your family and the relationships within it. Go two to three generations back, and note any information you have about

- the presence of any form of abuse
- history of illness
- history of substance abuse or addiction

Do you see any patterns in your family of origin?

_____

_____

_____

_____

_____

_____

_____

My Family Tree

What are your beliefs about what can be "passed down" in families?

_____

_____

_____

_____

_____

Reflect and write about the influence you believe your upbringing or the history of your family of origin has had on you.

_____

_____

_____

_____

_____

Relationship History

Reflect on your past relationships. Write a brief history of them. Go back as far as you can remember and record the name of the person, your age at the time of the relationship, and—using the information about abusive relationships from chapter 1—classify each as healthy, abusive, or uncertain.

_____

_____

_____

_____

_____

_____

_____

_____

Do you notice any patterns in your own relationships? What are they?

_____

_____

_____

_____

_____

_____

_____

_____

_____

Who were your relationship role models? What did you learn from them?

_____

_____

_____

_____

_____

_____

Imagine your ideal partner, boss, or family member—not a fantasy relationship, but your ideal.

_____

_____

_____

_____

_____

Record any lingering questions or doubts you may have about what you've been through in relationships.

_____

_____

_____

_____

_____

CHAPTER WRAP-UP

In this chapter, we took some of what we learned in chapter 1 to construct a portrait of your abusive relationship. Recalling what happened to you, when it occurred, and the most recent incident will help you put aside any previous denial or inclination to minimize the abuse. In the second half of this chapter, you had the opportunity to explore this abusive relationship in the context of your other life experiences, specifically your relationship history, family history, and any significant event during the time you were beginning your relationship with your abuser. This helps identify any vulnerabilities you may have had when becoming a target for this type of abuser.

PART II

Taking Action

IN CHAPTERS 1 THROUGH 3, WE EXPLORED what emotional abuse is and how we often manage its effects through survival mode for an extended period of time.

Survival mode, simply put, means we are *just trying to get through the day*. We have focused on minimizing our pain and suffering, and have tried to keep things on an even keel. It means making decisions based on trying to please and accommodate the abuser. Hopefully it's now understood that there is nothing you did to cause the abuse or the denial, minimization, and self-blame that you've operated from. These survival mechanisms kept you from feeling helpless. While they may have also helped decrease some of the conflict, they also probably contributed to you staying in the abusive situation. When we fully accept that we were being abused, did nothing to cause it, and cannot control the abusive person's behavior, we can begin to reconnect with ourselves and our loved ones, and break free.

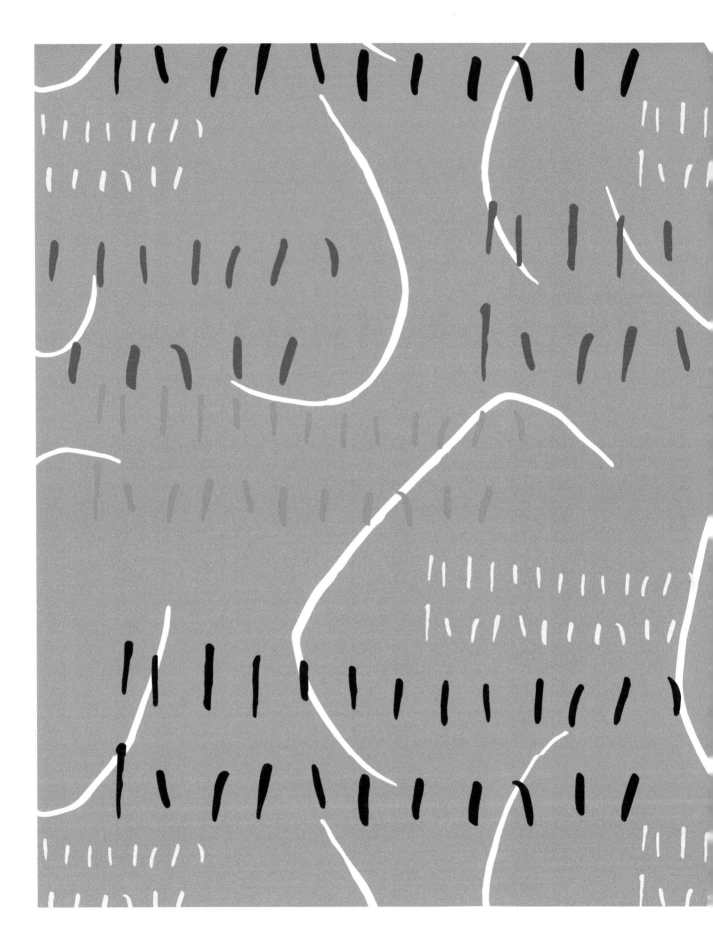

CHAPTER 4

Self-Compassion and Self-Care

S elf-compassion and self-care are vitally important for recovering from abuse. In this chapter, I ask you to turn your attention to your relationship with yourself. Up to this point we have spent a lot of time looking at your relationship to others; however, how we care for and relate to our own thoughts and feelings creates our internal environment. How we care for our bodies increases our resiliency. Whether we are talking about recovery from abuse or a mental health issue, physical self-care is underestimated in its importance to recovery.

Compassion is the ability to recognize the suffering of others, accompanied by a desire to ease that suffering. Compassion motivates us to do random acts of kindness, volunteer, give money to charities, or devote ourselves to caring for others in our lives. Compassion in all of its forms obviously makes the world a better place. Many of us find it easier to show compassion for others than for ourselves.

What is more challenging for you when things go wrong? Being self-compassionate or showing compassion to others?

Kristin Neff, a self-compassion researcher who was the first to use the term academically, defines the three elements of self-compassion:

1. treating yourself with kindness, or not participating in self-criticism
2. accepting yourself as a member of the human race or staying connected to the idea that we all make mistakes and experience pain
3. adopting a nonjudgmental awareness of experiences—also known as mindfulness

KEY ELEMENTS OF SELF-COMPASSION

Compassion and self-compassion can be cultivated. Keeping the three key elements in mind, adapted from Neff's research, doing the following exercises can start you on the path to cultivating self-compassion.

Becoming a Kind Friend to Yourself

Let's begin with the first element in the practice of self-compassion by thinking about yourself as your own best friend. Answer the following questions, and you will reflect later how this might change the relationship you have with yourself.

What does friendship look like to you?

_____

_____

_____

_____

_____

What is the trait you value most in a friend?

_____

_____

_____

_____

_____

Do you consider yourself a good friend? Why or why not?

_____

_____

_____

_____

_____

What makes you feel most loved?

_____

_____

_____

_____

_____

How can you apply your reflections on friendship to begin to shift your relationship with yourself?

_____

_____

_____

_____

_____

Name and describe two concrete things you can do today to practice self-compassion and become your own best friend.

_____

_____

_____

_____

A Letter to Myself

The way we treat ourselves is typically different from how we treat our friends and loved ones. We are more likely to take a harsh, critical tone in response to our own perceived mistakes. We may also hold ourselves back from taking risks, in anticipation of negative responses from others.

It's likely that the abuser in your life reinforced this fear. Emotional abuse often highlights and reinforces our worst fears about ourselves, as well as our deepest insecurities. It may require a bit of effort to change this, but it is worth it. Research confirms that self-criticism puts us at risk for depression. It becomes even more important in your recovery from abuse to recognize the absolute necessity to treat yourself with loving-kindness—the same loving-kindness we reserve for those people in our lives we hold most dear.

Write a letter to yourself and include an acknowledgment of your suffering, validation of your feelings about it, and words of love and encouragement.

_____

_____

_____

_____

_____

_____

_____

_____

_____

_____

_____

_____

_____

Next, sit in front of a mirror and read the letter out loud, pausing briefly at regular intervals to look at yourself. Take five minutes here to reflect on how you feel doing this exercise. Be mindful of any sensations in your body, as well as any resistance that comes up. Write about your reflections here.

_____

_____

_____

_____

_____

_____

_____

_____

_____

_____

_____

_____

_____

Acknowledging Your Humanity

The tendency toward perfectionism and self-criticism can result in overidentification with perceived mistakes. In this way we blame ourselves for our own suffering, and use it as evidence that we are bad, less than, or so different from others. Trauma survivors often describe themselves as outsiders and have difficulty seeing themselves as part of humanity. Acknowledging our own humanity means recognizing we all make mistakes, choose poorly, and fail sometimes. Regardless of the mistakes you believe you made you are not responsible for the abuse that you endured. It broadens our perspective when we can connect our experience to a shared human condition.

> Now let's uncover some of the harsh criticisms you may have experienced or are currently experiencing. Write out some of the negative self-talk that came up for you in the previous exercises.

_____

_____

_____

_____

_____

_____

_____

_____

_____

_____

_____

_____

_____

_____

Write out all the ways you have blamed yourself specifically for the abuse you have experienced. Use the sentence starters or write your own.

I _____

It's my fault because _____

If only _____

I shouldn't have _____

Take three of the statements you wrote in the previous sentence starters and write about them now from a mindfulness approach. Address the other components of self-compassion—acknowledging your own humanity and not judging, just acknowledging your thoughts or feelings.

Example:
Negative statement: I feel bad because I am bad.
Acknowledge your humanity: I am suffering. Everyone suffers.
Mindful noticing: I feel sorrow.

Negative statement: _____

Acknowledge your humanity: _____

Mindful noticing: _____

Negative statement: _____

Acknowledge your humanity: _____

Mindful noticing: _____

Negative statement: _____

Acknowledge your humanity: _____

Mindful noticing: _____

REFRAINING FROM JUDGMENT—MINDFULNESS

We often fight the feelings we experience as unpleasant, and we want to hold on to and extend the ones we experience as positive. We categorize and judge all of our feelings and experiences as good or bad, and that greatly determines how we feel about our lives, ourselves, and our future.

In my practice, I have often used the metaphor of *weather* for experiencing emotions. The weather can change from one hour to the next, from day to day, or from season to season, but when it rains we know it will not rain forever. The varying changes of weather are similar to our different emotional states. When strong emotions are present, a strong desire to act typically follows. This is where the impulse to distract, avoid, use substances, self-harm, or act out in some way might show up. If we practice a mindful approach, we acknowledge and observe, without action, much the way we would respond to the weather: "Oh, it's going to rain today." We accept the weather as a temporary thing we cannot change. In accepting this, we can refocus on how we take care of ourselves during this period, such as "I will bring my umbrella."

The next two exercises can help when you are feeling strong emotions or when you are feeling numb. To recover, victims of abuse need to become familiar with and embrace the sensations in their bodies. When you are afraid, you live in a body that is tense and on guard. These exercises can help you notice and then describe the feelings in your body. We are trying to focus not on the emotions here, but on the sensations, such as tightness, tingling, emptiness, and heat.

Body Scan to Increase Self-Awareness

Checking in with yourself at regular intervals is an important aspect of self-care. You have to know what you need to provide for yourself.

This exercise guides you to turn your attention to each part of your body to notice where you are experiencing sensations or holding tension.

Get into a comfortable position and move up through your whole body, beginning with your toes. Proceed slowly, being mindful of your breath.

After completing the first scan, repeat it, but this time notice where you find tension or pain. Write a reflection about what sensations you noticed and any thoughts or associations that emerged during this process.

_____

_____

_____

_____

_____

Progressive Muscle Relaxation

This exercise guides you to turn your attention to each part of your body to improve awareness and control of tension versus relaxation in your body.

Get into a comfortable position and move up through your whole body, beginning with your toes. Proceed slowly, being mindful of your breathing. Start with your feet, one at a time, and then move up through your body, alternating from the left side to the right side as you go. It may be difficult at first to isolate muscles, but this becomes easier with practice.

Step One

Take a slow, deep inhale, and squeeze the muscles in the part of the body you are focusing on. Do this as hard as you can for about five seconds. It is important to really feel the tension in your muscles. This may even cause a bit of discomfort, so be careful not to overdo it.

Step Two

After about five seconds of tension, let all the tightness flow out of the tensed muscles. Be sure to exhale as you do this step. You should feel the muscles become loose and limp as the tension flows out. It is important to very deliberately focus on and notice the difference between the tension and relaxation in your muscles. This is the most important part of the whole exercise.

Foot—Curl your toes downward.

Lower leg and foot—Tighten your calf muscle by pulling your toes toward you.

Upper leg—Squeeze your thigh muscles.

Hand—Clench your fist.

Entire right arm—Tighten your biceps by drawing your forearm up toward your shoulder and flexing the muscle, while clenching your fist.

Buttocks—Tighten the muscles by pulling your buttocks together.

Stomach—Suck in your stomach.

Chest—Tighten it by taking a deep breath.

Neck and shoulders—Raise your shoulders up to touch your ears.

Mouth—Open your mouth wide enough to stretch the hinges of your jaw.

Eyes—Clench your eyelids shut.

Forehead—Raise your eyebrows.

After completing this exercise, notice how you are feeling. Are you more relaxed from head to toe? Are you more aware of your body sensations after completing this exercise? Is there a noticeable difference in your body before and after the exercise?

_____

_____

_____

_____

_____

Diaphragmatic Breathing

Your diaphragm is the muscle that sits beneath your rib cage that separates your chest from your abdomen. You can engage your diaphragm more fully by pushing your belly out when you inhale and pulling your belly in to exhale, being mindful to release all the breath before your next inhale. It is best to practice breathing from your diaphragm for at least five minutes at a time, multiple times each day. It may help to attach this practice to other routines, such as waking up in the morning or going to sleep in bed, before or after meals, or when getting into or out of your car.

You can practice this type of breathing anywhere and in any position.

Mind-Body Connection to Self-Care

It's useful to consider the mind-body connection. Self-care—the idea of taking care of your body and physical health in combination with practicing stress management—has been a widespread topic and trend in recent years. This exercise explores our practices of self-care and introduces new ways to take care of ourselves during difficult moments.

What comes to mind when you think of self-care?

_____

_____

_____

Let's expand and support our present and future efforts toward increased self-care. When I begin working with a new client, it is my standard practice to assess how they take care of themselves and to get a baseline of their current practices to see if there is room for improvement. I am going to ask the same of you here. If you are just emerging from an abusive relationship, I suspect that you are experiencing some neglect because you have not been prioritizing your own needs. I have broken aspects of self-care into the following 13 categories, but feel free to add anything else that you feel is important and has not been adequately addressed. Answer each of the questions by circling Yes or No. Use this list to generate goals for the next activity.

SPIRITUAL PRACTICES

Do you go to church or belong to a spiritual community? **Yes/No**

Do you meditate? **Yes/No**

Do you read or study subjects you find inspirational or inspiring? **Yes/No**

Are you a part of a 12-step community? **Yes/No**

Do you take time to reflect? **Yes/No**

Do you enjoy nature, art, or music? **Yes/No**

Exploring Spirituality

Many people I work with don't feel certain about their spiritual beliefs, and many have rejected their religious upbringing, while others have embraced it. Our religious beliefs can sometimes hinder our perceptions of the abuse we experienced. Traditional gender roles or ideas about selflessness and altruism may confuse our assumptions regarding our abuser, or those who mistreat or take advantage of us.

While we value generosity, kindness, patience, and forgiveness, it can be difficult to sort out how we translate that to living day-to-day, particularly in the context of abusive relationships. Exploring spirituality means asking yourself some tough questions. However, spiritual practices, religious and otherwise, tend to promote hope and faith—two things that can greatly enhance our daily life and ability to cope.

NUTRITION

Are you aware of your diet? **Yes/No**

Do you eat at regular intervals? **Yes/No**

Are your food choices healthy? **Yes/No**

Do you eat enough fresh fruits and vegetables? **Yes/No**

Do you drink enough water? **Yes/No**

EXERCISE

Do you get enough exercise in a typical week? **Yes/No**

Are you sedentary in your day-to-day activities? **Yes/No**

Do you work out? At the gym? At home? **Yes/No**

Do you attend group exercise classes? **Yes/No**

Do you take walks with your dog or your children? **Yes/No**

SOCIAL ENGAGEMENT

Do you engage in fun activities with other people? **Yes/No**

Do you spend time with friends? **Yes/No**

Are you making new friends? **Yes/No**

Do you keep in touch with old friends? **Yes/No**

Do you engage in stimulating conversation with others? **Yes/No**

SOCIAL SUPPORTS

Do you express your feelings to people close to you? **Yes/No**

Do you ask for help when you need it? **Yes/No**

Do you spend time with people you love and trust? **Yes/No**

LIFESTYLE CHOICES

Do you smoke or vape? **Yes/No**

Do you engage in drug and alcohol use? **Yes/No**

Do you practice safe sex? **Yes/No**

SLEEP

Do you get seven to eight hours of sleep each night? **Yes/No**

Do you have consistent sleep routines? **Yes/No**

Do you experience sleep disturbances? **Yes/No**

Sleep Hygiene

We know how important sleep is to mental and physical health. Here we explore sleep hygiene as it relates to difficulty falling asleep or staying asleep.

Keeping a bedtime routine; limiting alcohol, caffeine, and nicotine use (especially close to bedtime); maintaining a dark and quiet environment; practicing aromatherapy, progressive muscle relaxation, and diaphragmatic breathing; and using a guided meditation app are all strategies that can support improved sleep. A yoga posture I have found effective for insomnia requires putting your legs up against a wall while lying flat on your back.

You will likely have to try several of these strategies to see what works for you. If ruminative thoughts, strong emotions, or intrusive memories are keeping you up at night, try keeping a worry journal or a dream journal. Also, talk about your traumatic experiences with a trusted friend, family member, or therapist. Those things we don't acknowledge in the daylight can often invade our sleep.

ATTENDING TO HEALTH ISSUES

Do you participate in preventive medical care? **Yes/No**

Do you seek medical or alternative treatments when you are not well? **Yes/No**

Do you take time off work when you are sick? **Yes/No**

PERSONAL HYGIENE

Do you attend to your personal hygiene on a daily basis? **Yes/No**

Do you wear clothing that is comfortable and suitable to your environment? **Yes/No**

Do you wear clothes that make you feel confident? **Yes/No**

PROFESSIONAL OR EDUCATIONAL PURSUITS

Are you in a job, career, or field of study that you find satisfying or interesting? **Yes/No**

Are you able to say no to excessive tasks or responsibilities? **Yes/No**

Can you advocate for yourself in the workplace/school? **Yes/No**

Do you have supportive relationships in your work/school environment? **Yes/No**

Are you learning new things related to your interests and values? **Yes/No**

Do you take breaks at work? **Yes/No**

Do you bring your work home? **Yes/No**

Do you take time off when you need it? **Yes/No**

HOBBIES

Do you have hobbies? **Yes/No**

Do you engage in those hobbies often? How often? **Yes/No**

Are they social in nature? **Yes/No**

Are they solitary in nature? **Yes/No**

ATTENTION TO PHYSICAL ENVIRONMENT

Do you have what you need in your home to meet your daily needs? **Yes/No**

Do you feel safe in your neighborhood and home? **Yes/No**

Is your living space tidy and organized? **Yes/No**

EMOTIONAL SELF-CARE

Do you speak to yourself kindly and compassionately? **Yes/No**

Do you accept love from others? **Yes/No**

Do you engage in comforting activities? **Yes/No**

Do you laugh or find reasons to laugh? **Yes/No**

SCHEDULE SHORT-TERM AND LONG-TERM NEEDS

Routines are great for stabilizing your mood and continuing to manage your day-to-day life during this difficult period. By attending to our short- and long-term needs, we minimize anxiety, stretch out our tasks over time, and remember to take care of ourselves in both big and small ways.

Get a wall calendar or an appointment book, or use a smartphone calendar, and begin to create a schedule for yourself and attend to your short-term and long-term needs. Start with today—make a to-do list, then look at what needs to be accomplished in the rest of your week. Regular checkups, teeth cleaning, and vaccinations for kids or pets are all important and contribute to our sense of control, competence, and stability.

Move on to keep track of the things you do every day, week, month, every three months, every six months, and annually. Think about important upcoming events for each month that you can put on your calendar to organize. Write down your sister's birthday in January, a trip planned in February, tax deadlines in March, and so on throughout the year. The focus here is progress, not perfection.

SMART GOALS FOR SELF-CARE

The SMART goals acronym was first introduced by George Doran in his 1981 article, "There's a S.M.A.R.T. Way to Write Management's Goals and Objectives." It is a widely taught and used framework for constructing achievable goals.

SMART stands for "specific, measurable, achievable, relevant, and time-bound."

Now revisit each category and prioritize the aspects that you believe are most important for your self-care at this time. Then let's set three goals for improving self-care:

1. _____

   S _____

   M _____

   A _____

   R _____

   T _____

2. _____

   S _____

   M _____

   A _____

   R _____

   T _____

3. _____

   S _____

   M _____

   A _____

   R _____

   T _____

How does your own experience of suffering affect your capacity to practice self-care? Identify and reflect on the obstacles you may encounter while establishing a self-care routine.

_____

_____

_____

_____

_____

_____

_____

CHAPTER WRAP-UP

Attention to self-care and self-compassion in this chapter addresses our ongoing physical, emotional, mental, and spiritual needs during this time of recovery. In this chapter, you assessed your current practices, built new skills, and set goals. Using the structure of the self-compassion exercises, you learned how to improve your relationship with yourself. Regular practice will provide the opportunity to turn from a self-critic into a loving friend. The self-care portion is crucial for recovery and going on to live a healthy and balanced life, one in which your own needs are a priority. A focus on health, organization, relaxation, mental stimulation, and purpose expands the possibilities for growth and satisfaction in your life.

CHAPTER 5

Boundaries

The previous chapter focused on self-care and highlighted its importance in recovery and beyond. But unlike the more obvious aspects of self-care, like healthy eating and exercise, setting healthy boundaries is difficult for most people to understand and practice.

I direct you back to the section entitled "How Did You Survive Your Relationship?" in chapter 2 (see page 22). Is there a connection between surviving the abuse and your level of ability to care for yourself? You learned to cope with or adapt to your abuse and shifted your focus from self to other, getting out of touch with your own needs and desires in the process. Adapting to the abuse tends to bleed into other relationships, because abuse affects how we feel about ourselves over time. The more we focus on others, the more disconnected we may get from ourselves. It can be harder to practice self-care, including establishing boundaries, because we just don't know what we need and have no real separation from others.

Healthy boundaries are a crucial component of self-care, so much so that this chapter is dedicated to boundaries—what they are, how to define your own personal boundaries, and how to implement boundaries in your daily life. There are many benefits to setting healthy boundaries, including helping us make decisions based on what is best for us, not just for the people around us.

Difficulty setting or maintaining boundaries in personal and work relationships can lead to resentment, anger, burnout, financial burdens, and wasted time. It also sets us up for being taken advantage of by others. Let's explore what you might already know about this topic.

WHAT IS A BOUNDARY?

Boundaries define space, protect us, keep things in or out of our space, and define our ownership or responsibility. The first step in establishing and setting boundaries is examining how boundaries currently function in your life.

I invite you to think now about other types of boundaries—walls, fences, gates, doors, windows, and screens are all boundaries human beings recognize and navigate. Boundaries can be rigid and locked, or loose and penetrable.

In this chapter, we are examining personal boundaries. We look at your family of origin, as well as your current relationships. The tasks in this chapter help you define, clarify, and enforce your personal boundaries.

Personal boundaries are the guidelines that we use in our relationships to help us define safe and comfortable ways of interacting with others. They help us define where we stop and others begin and help us protect and take care of ourselves.

Healthy boundaries help us establish our sense of identity, define our individuality, and clarify what we will and will not hold ourselves responsible for. Boundaries are psychological, emotional, and physical. For example, saying no to physical contact from a coworker sets a physical boundary that is just as important as setting the emotional boundary of asking that coworker not to make unreasonable demands on your time or emotions.

Healthy boundaries at work can help us find more satisfaction and experience less stress. Saying no is an obvious way to set a boundary, but how many times have you felt the need to explain or even make something up to justify saying no? You do not need to explain; overexplaining or compromising your values is counter to setting boundaries. It is your right to decide what you do and don't do.

Exploring Boundaries in Your Family of Origin

We first learned about boundaries within our families. This exercise can help illuminate our understanding of how our personal boundaries developed. While looking back at your experiences growing up in your family, answer the following questions.

PAST

Looking back now at your family of origin, did your family have and respect one another's boundaries? Reflect and describe.

_____

_____

_____

_____

_____

_____

_____

_____

How do you think these early experiences affected the way you currently manage boundaries in your relationships? Reflect and describe.

_____

_____

_____

_____

_____

_____

_____

_____

PRESENT

In the next exercise, we look at your current boundaries and patterns in relationships.

Rate yourself on the following statements using a scale from 1 to 4.

1—never   **2**—sometimes   **3**—frequently   **4**—always

1. I have trouble saying no. _____
2. People in my life assume I am always available to them. _____
3. It's hard to find time for myself. _____
4. I don't tell people when they have hurt me. _____
5. I don't tell people when I feel angry with them. _____
6. People use my stuff without asking. _____
7. I compromise my values to avoid anger or rejection. _____
8. I do not express my own opinion if I think others would not agree. _____
9. Sometimes I don't know what I want, feel, or need. _____
10. I struggle with decision-making. _____

> **Look now at the previous exercise and which statements you answered with "frequently" and "always." Take some time to reflect on and write about whether you believe people in your life are violating your boundaries. Who are these people? How are they violating you and your boundaries?**

_____

_____

_____

_____

_____

_____

_____

_____

_____

_____

_____

_____

_____

_____

OBSTRUCTIONS TO BOUNDARY SETTING

It may not always be obvious to us that a specific attitude or belief contributes to the problems in our lives. We need to claim our attitudes and beliefs because they fall within our control, and we are the only ones who can change them.

The difficulty lies in the fact that we often learn these attitudes and beliefs early and implicitly in life. Those of us with boundary problems usually have distorted beliefs about responsibility. We may feel responsible for others or hold others responsible for our feelings and choices. So far in this chapter, it may seem as if the individual who has difficulty setting limits is the one who has the boundary problem. However, those who don't respect the boundaries of others also have boundary problems. The person who can't say no may have boundary problems, but those who do not respect others' boundaries or ignore the needs of others have them, too. Remember from the descriptions of abusers in chapter 1 that abusers frequently will not take no for an answer and will use a variety of tactics to dominate, control, and reinforce their victims' difficulty in setting boundaries.

Exploring Myths about Boundaries

In this exercise, we explore some myths about boundaries. Our underlying beliefs regarding interpersonal boundaries and responsibility define our actions, whether or not we are consciously aware of them. Sometimes there is a disconnect between what we think and how we feel. For example, a friend may request a favor we think asks too much of us. We think about saying no; however, we end up feeling guilty. In the context of emotional abuse, inadequate boundaries are a setup for being taken advantage of or, worse, not noticing we are being repeatedly violated by a significant other.

Checkmark the items on the following checklists that you feel apply to you.

Common myths about boundaries:

☐ If I set boundaries, I'm being selfish.

☐ Setting boundaries or saying no is an expression of disobedience or disrespect.

☐ If I begin setting boundaries, I will be hurt by others.

☐ If I set boundaries, I will hurt others.

☐ Boundaries are an expression of anger.

☐ When others set boundaries, it injures me.

☐ Boundaries make me feel guilty.

☐ Boundaries are permanent.

☐ I will lose people or things if I begin to set boundaries.

Behaviors that may signal boundary problems:

☐ telling everyone everything

☐ speaking intimately with someone you just met

☐ going against personal values or rights to please others

- [ ] letting others describe your reality
- [ ] allowing others to define you
- [ ] feeling overwhelmed by another person
- [ ] accepting food, gifts, touch, or sex that you don't want
- [ ] letting others direct your life
- [ ] falling in love with anyone who shows interest, or someone you just met
- [ ] not noticing when someone else displays inappropriate boundaries
- [ ] not noticing when someone violates your boundaries
- [ ] giving as much as you can for the sake of giving
- [ ] allowing someone to take as much as they can from you
- [ ] taking as much as you can from someone else for the sake of getting

If you answered yes to any of these questions, you are experiencing difficulty with boundaries. Use this exercise to assist you in determining where you may be vulnerable and to help you explore possible behavior changes these items might suggest. For example, if you answered yes to "telling everyone everything," it suggests you may need to allow more time in getting to know people before trusting them with your personal information.

DEFINING AND ESTABLISHING PERSONAL BOUNDARIES

In the previous exercises, we explored the possible roots and manifestations of dysfunctional boundaries. Another obvious connection here is that our boundaries may have been confused, compromised, or deeply diminished by our emotionally abusive relationship. Recovery from abuse includes a good deal of focus on rebuilding our boundaries and identity.

In this next series of exercises, we focus on how to rebuild. I ask you to look at your values and culture, your current relationships, and how to set boundaries using assertive communication.

Values Exploration

In the next exercises, we examine what's important to you, as well as the personal attributes and behaviors you value.

Use the following list to identify 20 things that you value. Rank these values from 1 to 20. This is not an exhaustive list, so feel free to add to it, or swap a value listed for one of your own.

☐ family relationships

☐ friendships

☐ community involvement

☐ political involvement

☐ recreation

☐ belonging to a spiritual or religious community

☐ adhering to a particular way of eating

☐ physical fitness

☐ being in an intimate relationship

☐ career

☐ success

☐ wealth

☐ protecting the environment

☐ arts

☐ cleanliness

☐ being fashionable

☐ home environment (physical)

☐ volunteering for causes

☐ caring for animals

☐ education

☐ _____

☐ _____

☐ _____

Consider the previous exercise and answer the following questions:

Was this a difficult exercise for you? Why or why not?

_____

_____

_____

_____

_____

_____

Do you think you have been living in alignment with your values? Why or why not?

_____

_____

_____

_____

_____

_____

_____

How has your experience in an abusive relationship affected your values and your ability to live in alignment with them?

_____

_____

_____

_____

_____

_____

_____

Another aspect of values is personal qualities. Who do you want to be in the world? What are the personal qualities you most admire in others?

_____

_____

_____

_____

_____

_____

_____

_____

What are three qualities you like about yourself?

_____

_____

_____

_____

_____

_____

_____

How has your abusive relationship affected this area of your life or identity?

_____

_____

_____

_____

_____

_____

_____

_____

_____

_____

In this section, write out specific behaviors that make you feel neutral/pleasant or distressed. This can include things like being touched by others, someone eating food off your plate, or someone dropping by your house without calling. Spend some time with this exercise, and think of as many things as you can.

Neutral/Pleasant _____ Distressed _____

_____

_____

_____

_____

_____

You may have realized in completing the previous exercise that your boundaries and comfort level with certain behaviors change in different relationships. In the next exercise, to clarify how "close" you feel to people in your world, trace the three circles below. Each circle signifies a level of relationship closeness. Write your name in the inner circle, and ask yourself the following questions:

Who is in there with me, if anyone?

_____

_____

Now add outer layers, and place people in your world in each circle as you feel appropriate. Where do you put other people in your life?

_____

_____

IMPLEMENTING BOUNDARIES

These exercises were meant to help you clarify your boundaries. The next set of exercises is designed to help you begin setting these boundaries in your relationships.

Boundaries are universally necessary in all of our relationships. It's important for partners to understand and respect each other's boundaries in a long-term partnership. Boundaries in the workplace are just as necessary as those in our personal relationships, and it is also important to respect and be respected by people you don't know.

A client who is a manager in her workplace recently shared with me a difficult moment she experienced with her staff. A colleague told her that a staff member's personal information was discussed in a shared workspace. The conversation included some disturbing details and made it difficult for others to concentrate on their work.

The manager practiced setting boundaries—consulting and reviewing policies and procedures of appropriate workplace behavior, and followed up with the staff, addressing concerns about confidentiality and safety in the workplace.

This can be a much more challenging situation to manage when there is a power differential. What if the offender is the boss, and others could fear retaliation if they sought assistance? We get a little deeper into this in the next chapter, which focuses on safety planning. This is a good illustration of the importance of having open and honest conversations with people in your life about your boundaries and theirs.

Styles of Communication

We can divide most communication into three categories—passive, assertive, and aggressive. Thinking back to chapter 1, we can probably identify the methods used most frequently by abusers as passive—or passive-aggressive—and aggressive. If we ever used assertive communication in our abusive relationship, it was frequently used against us. Assertive communication—focused on the use of "I" statements—is the cleanest and clearest communication style we can engage in.

I feel _____ when _____

And it would help if _____

It might sound something like this:

I feel criticized and embarrassed when you make jokes at my expense in front of my family. It would help me if you didn't make me the target of your jokes.

I feel worried when you are not home by 7 p.m., and it would help me worry less if you would text me when you will be late.

Pick one situation in your life to practice "I" statements. Write about your experience here:

_____

_____

_____

_____

_____

TIPS ON SETTING BOUNDARIES

Be assertive—Use "I" statements, and speak openly and honestly about your preferences. Additionally, be clear with your responses. If someone asks a favor that you cannot afford to give, don't say "Maybe" or "Let me get back to you," or avoid the person. Say "No" and don't feel the need to provide an excuse. You have the right to say no.

Know your values—Make decisions based on your personal values, as highlighted in previous exercises. Living out of alignment with our values creates internal conflict and anxiety.

Keep the focus on yourself—Don't say "Stop bothering me." Instead, say "I need some alone time now. I will let you know when I'm free."

Know your limits—Don't give more than you can afford to give, physically, emotionally, and mentally.

Listen to your emotions—Notice your overall comfort level, including any budding resentment or anger. These are clear indications that someone is violating your boundaries.

Consider the whole relationship—Some days or weeks you may give more, and other times you may give less. Consider the whole relationship when evaluating your relationships. Are you always the one who gives?

We have mostly been discussing the difficulty of saying no and failing to assert our boundaries with others. However, sometimes when we have been in an abusive relationship, we find ourselves changed. It may feel like the right thing to do is to establish rigid boundaries with others. We may decide that we cannot trust anyone and start keeping everyone at a physical and/or emotional distance. Overly rigid boundaries can be just as problematic as overly loose boundaries. We need to reestablish healthy relationships in recovery that support our growth and help us feel connected, loved, and supported.

Codependency

The working definition of codependency that I use with my clients recovering from abuse is "the tendency to set aside your own needs to control the dysfunctional abusive behavior of a significant other."

Co-Dependents Anonymous, or CoDA, identifies categories of behavior patterns that define codependency. These categories are denial, low self-esteem, compliance, control, and avoidance.

Some examples of the behaviors or tendencies identified in the categories listed include:

- [ ] difficulty identifying feelings
- [ ] perceiving themselves as unselfish and dedicated to the well-being of others
- [ ] the belief that they can take care of themselves without help
- [ ] a tendency to mask pain
- [ ] an inability to recognize emotional unavailability in others
- [ ] difficulty making decisions
- [ ] being self-critical

Collage of My Personal Boundaries

This exercise gives you the opportunity to visualize and concretize your personal boundaries and standards for relationships. Focus on that which strengthens you and promotes a sense of resolve in caring for yourself in a relationship. On a large piece of paper, trace or draw an outline of yourself, or the general outline of a person. Draw pictures or cut out pictures from magazines and place them inside the outline. Use images or words that reflect what is unique about you. Think about

- [ ] embarrassed by recognition
- [ ] do not perceive themselves as lovable
- [ ] loyal and remain in harmful situations too long
- [ ] compromise their own values and integrity
- [ ] put aside their own interests
- [ ] hypervigilant to the feelings of others
- [ ] afraid to express their own beliefs and opinions
- [ ] accept sexual attention when what they really want is love
- [ ] allow addictions
- [ ] use indirect or evasive communication to avoid conflict
- [ ] suppress their own feelings

This is not a complete list, but if you want to learn more, visit CODA.org.

colors or symbols you love or identify with, or images that are meaningful to you. When determining where to place images on the representation of your body, think about what you love about that part of your body and the function it serves, specific to you and not just general function. For example, inside the outline of the hands, you may represent your ability to provide nourishment, affection, or self-care. Then move outside the outline and write the interpersonal boundaries that you identified in this chapter, using simple sentences. An alternative to writing out your boundaries can be the creation of a personal "Bill of Rights."

CHAPTER WRAP-UP

Boundaries are one of the most important topics in this workbook. They are the guidelines we use to navigate our relationships. It is likely that your boundaries have been systematically compromised by your involvement with an abusive significant other.

In this chapter, we explored the definition of boundaries and how boundaries are influenced and developed in our families of origin. We reviewed what has interfered with establishing and practicing boundaries, including investigating myths. Clarifying the past is useful and helps set the course for the future. The remainder of the chapter provided an opportunity to review values and current relationships, and construct a new set of boundaries and expectations. Finally, it outlined tools for implementing these boundaries, using communication strategies and tips for doing so. Return to this chapter when you experience self-doubt or confusion regarding a relationship and need clarity. The last activity is designed to help you visualize and actualize your newfound boundaries, and you may want to revisit it from time to time.

CHAPTER 6

A Safety Plan

No matter where you are in your relationship, planning for your emotional and physical safety is extremely important. The primary reason a *safety plan* is so important is because when you decide to leave an abusive partner whose main goal is to dominate and control you, an escalation of controlling and abusive behaviors is likely and typical. Consequently, when the abuser begins to suspect that you are trying to leave, the abuse will likely become worse and may even escalate to physical violence.

So leaving an abusive relationship is potentially the riskiest, most dangerous time for the victim. Aside from inflicting physical abuse, an abuser may take away access to money or transportation, hide important documents, or seek legal action against you in one form or another to try to protect their own interests. Whether it's accusing you of abuse, child neglect, or a severe mental illness, the abuser typically escalates situations to maintain control.

Some of the material here may seem extreme or frightening; however, escalation is typical and therefore predictable. I am going to ask you here to try to remember some of the more painful or frightening aspects of the abuse.

Assessing Danger

The following questions are intended to support you in assessing your safety and danger in relation to leaving the abusive situation. While prediction can be tricky, it has been my experience that threats should be given serious consideration. Most of the individuals I have worked with have reported a strong sense of what their abusive partners are capable of—even if there has been little or no violence in the relationship. Research has shown that certain behaviors and conditions dramatically increase risk of harm to victims. These include the use of a weapon or threatening with a weapon, threatening to kill the victim and children, choking a victim, constant jealousy and control of daily activities, spying on the victim, if the victim has made previous attempts to leave, if the abuser is unemployed, a history of suicide attempts by the abuser, abuse of children, substance abuse problems, and interference with 911 calls. I encourage anyone with even the slightest indication of danger to consult a professional to aid in your risk assessment.

Has your abuser ever made threats if you were to leave them? Write them here.

_____

_____

_____

_____

What are your thoughts and feelings about these threats? Do you believe this person is capable of carrying out their threats?

_____

_____

_____

_____

_____

WHAT IS A SAFETY PLAN?

Even if this person has never been physical with you but has made repeated threats to harm you in some fundamental way if you were to leave, trust your instincts but proceed with the utmost caution. This is no time to minimize or second-guess yourself.

Consider the following steps before you leave, as you leave, or after you leave an abusive partner, to protect your physical, emotional, and mental well-being.

1. Get the support of a friend, family member, neighbor, or abuse professional. Use hotlines and local agencies to plan how you will leave safely.
2. Make a safety plan. A safety plan can address any of your needs at any stage of the relationship abuse.

A safety plan is a personalized and practical plan that includes ways to remain safe while in a relationship, when planning to leave the relationship, or after you leave the relationship. Safety planning involves detailing what tangible things you will need, how to cope with the strong mixed emotions associated with leaving, identifying support people, taking legal action, and more. A good safety plan is tailored to your unique situation, with all the vital information you need.

Some of the things in your safety plan may seem obvious; however, it's important to remember that in moments of fear or crisis, our brains don't function like they do when we are calm. Having a safety plan laid out in advance can help you protect yourself in those stressful moments. A planned exit is preferable to an exit in the middle of a conflict, which may serve to escalate your abuser's behavior. When you are planning to leave, begin to do the following:

- Keep any evidence of abuse, such as pictures of injuries, texts, emails, and so on.
- Keep a journal of the abusive incidents, noting dates, events, and threats made. Keep your journal in a safe place where your abuser cannot locate it.
- Know where you can go to get help.
- Tell someone what is happening to you, access support, and enlist help.
- If you have children, identify a safe place for them, like a room with a lock or a friend's house where they can go for help. Reassure them that their job is to stay safe, not to protect you.

- Try to set money aside, or ask friends or family members to hold money for you. Do this discreetly, so as not to alert the abusive partner.
- Decide where you can go when you leave, and arrange the means to get there.
- Gather important items and documents or copies of important papers:
    - birth certificate and children's birth certificates
    - Social Security cards
    - financial information
    - money and/or credit cards (in your name)
    - copies of any lease or rental agreements, or the deed to your home
    - car registration and insurance papers
    - health and life insurance papers
    - medical records for you and your children
    - school records
    - work permits/green card/visa
    - passport
    - divorce and custody papers
    - marriage license
    - medications
    - extra set of house and car keys
    - valuable jewelry
    - pictures and sentimental items
    - several changes of clothes for you and your children

If you find yourself separated from your cell phone, make sure you have phone numbers written down somewhere else, and include:

- the phone numbers and email addresses for local domestic violence programs or shelters
- contact information for friends, relatives, and family members

AFTER YOU LEAVE

- Cut off contact with your ex if you can.
- Resist the urge to look your abuser up on social media. Unfriend or block them, and if pictures and news keep popping up, it could be helpful to remove mutual friends as well.
- Change your locks, and block the abuser's number if applicable.

- Change your work hours and the route you take to work.
- If you have a restraining order, keep a certified copy of it with you at all times, and inform friends, neighbors, employers, or school personnel that you have a restraining order in effect.
- Consider renting a post office box or using the address of a friend for your mail. Be aware that addresses are on restraining orders and police reports, and be careful to whom you give your address and phone number.
- Reschedule appointments that the abusive partner is aware of.
- Change your routines and be aware of your surroundings.
- Alert neighbors and request that they call the police if they feel you may be in danger.
- Tell your coworkers or classmates about the situation.

Be aware that all the suggestions and guidelines offered here are general. I strongly recommend enlisting the support of professionals when you are leaving an abusive relationship to appropriately plan for safety, if there is any risk of danger.

During the healing process, you may feel the need to offer forgiveness, help your abusive partner through the breakup, or show them how you're better off now. Counterintuitive as it may seem, it's actually more difficult to get closure and begin healing without severing all ties.

After you have left and further ensured your safety, allow yourself to get help and support from others. Spend time with friends and family who care about you. Tell them what you need from them, whether that's someone to talk to about what you went through, or someone to keep you from answering phone calls from your abuser, texting them back, or using any other form of communication.

In the preceding chapters of this book, there are detailed exercises and information to aid you in your healing journey. Review those now. Remember that it's not your fault. Educate yourself about the abuse, understand how it happened, take credit for the strength and resilience it has taken you to get this far, and practice self-care and self-compassion.

The saying "time heals all wounds" can be incredibly frustrating, but there is some truth in it. Healing and overcoming abuse takes work and conscious effort. Recovery takes time, space, and energy. Give yourself as much time as you need to heal.

Recovery looks different for everyone, and each person has to find what works for them.

Identify and Work Toward Achievable Goals

Using the SMART goals introduced in chapter 4 (see page 70), write one or more personal goals you have now that you have left the relationship. SMART stands for specific, measurable, achievable, relevant, and time-bound.

1. _____

    S _____

    M _____

    A _____

    R _____

    T _____

2. _____

    S _____

    M _____

    A _____

    R _____

    T _____

Create a Peaceful Space for Yourself

Choose a place in your house, in a public space, or in nature that feels safe and peaceful to you. Write in detail everything that you want it to have, including items that appeal to the senses. For example, a scented candle and soft music might be items you feel are necessary in creating an atmosphere that promotes a sense of calm and relaxation.

_____

_____

_____

_____

_____

_____

_____

Remind Yourself of Your Great Value

Adopt a new practice for yourself. Gratitude journals and affirmations are two examples you might try. Remember the reality that you are an important and valuable human being; this is so beneficial for your emotional health. It is never your fault when someone chooses to abuse you, and it has no reflection on the great value you have as a person.

Give yourself emotional breaks, and step back from your situation sometimes. In the end, this can help give you the space and clarity to make the decisions that are best for you. Don't talk about it and think about it all the time. Allow yourself to enjoy other aspects of your life.

Consider the significant relationships, work, values, and self-care practices you have identified so far in this book. Give a "slice" on this pie diagram to each important area of your life:

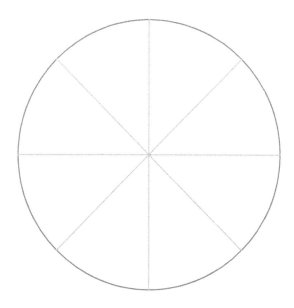

My Safety Plan

Now let's design a personalized safety plan for you. Using the information from this chapter, make an individualized safety plan. Access your personal and professional supports, and write out all the steps you need to take to move forward safely.

Because I am still in my relationship, I will manage my safety by

_____

_____

_____

_____

_____

Because I am preparing to leave the relationship, I will need to plan for

_____

_____

_____

_____

_____

Because I have left the relationship and I am considering going back, I

_____

_____

_____

_____

_____

I am free and clear of the relationship, but I am struggling with strong feelings that can be difficult to manage, such as

_____

_____

_____

_____

_____

I will know I am healed when

_____

_____

_____

_____

_____

I will know I am ready to love again or just date when

_____

_____

_____

_____

_____

Restraining Orders

A restraining order or protective order is a legal document that can be obtained through court and is used to protect a person in a situation involving domestic violence, assault, harassment, stalking, or sexual assault. In the United States, every state has some form of domestic violence restraining order law, and many states also have specific restraining order laws for stalking and sexual assault.

Restraining and personal protection order laws vary from state to state. All states establish who can file orders, what protection you can expect from the order, and how it will be enforced. The order will establish limits and boundaries around the abuser's behavior toward you. Abusers are ordered to stay a certain distance away from the victim, their home, their workplace or their school, and are ordered not to contact them. Sometimes victims request that the court order include all possible methods of contact, including texts, calls, mail, fax, email, or delivery of flowers, gifts, or notes.

The evidence needed to obtain these orders varies from court to court. If you are able to get an order of protection, keep it with you at all times. In one previous client's case, she bumped into her ex at a large public venue five years after the relationship ended. He immediately reengaged her abusively, launching into a string of insults and curses. She had that order in her purse (never left home without it), tracked down a police officer, and had him arrested on the spot.

If you think you might benefit from a restraining order, seek professional support. Domestic violence services in your local community can guide you through this process.

CHAPTER WRAP-UP

This chapter focused on safety and deconstructed the key elements to manage your current situation. Assessing potential for danger will guide how we proceed through the steps that follow. Even if you determine there is no physical threat to your safety, I urge you to proceed carefully and establish steps to be taken based on minimizing your risk of having any feelings of anger or frustration at your abuser. Acting on feelings of anger or frustration may result in an escalation of control tactics at minimum. Carefully consider the items identified in this chapter, specifically, what you may need both practically and emotionally to move forward from this period of your life. In the latter part of this chapter, I took you through the steps to create a personalized safety plan and set goals for your future. Don't skip over the sections that focus on healing, namely, creating a calm place for yourself and giving time and energy to the other parts of your life, as these items are vital to your recovery.

PART III

Moving Forward

IN THIS SECTION, WE MAP out your next steps. Whether you are in the process of leaving your abusive relationship or have already done so, you are probably thinking, well, what now? How long will it take to recover from this experience? What will replace it? You may find yourself with a hole in your life where the abusive relationship was. I believe that if we are not intentional about what will fill that void, we risk repeating old patterns.

The following chapters are designed to help you with that intentionality. I hope to increase your consciousness of your own behavior, as well as that of others. There are obvious clues to character traits, personal qualities, and behaviors in our brief interactions with others, as long as we trust our senses and stay present in our interactions. Negative experiences and learned biases can interfere with our ability to read social situations, and can affect the quality of our relationships and the people we accept into our lives.

Take your time moving through these chapters. Mindfulness—being present in the here and now—is your best guide for what comes next.

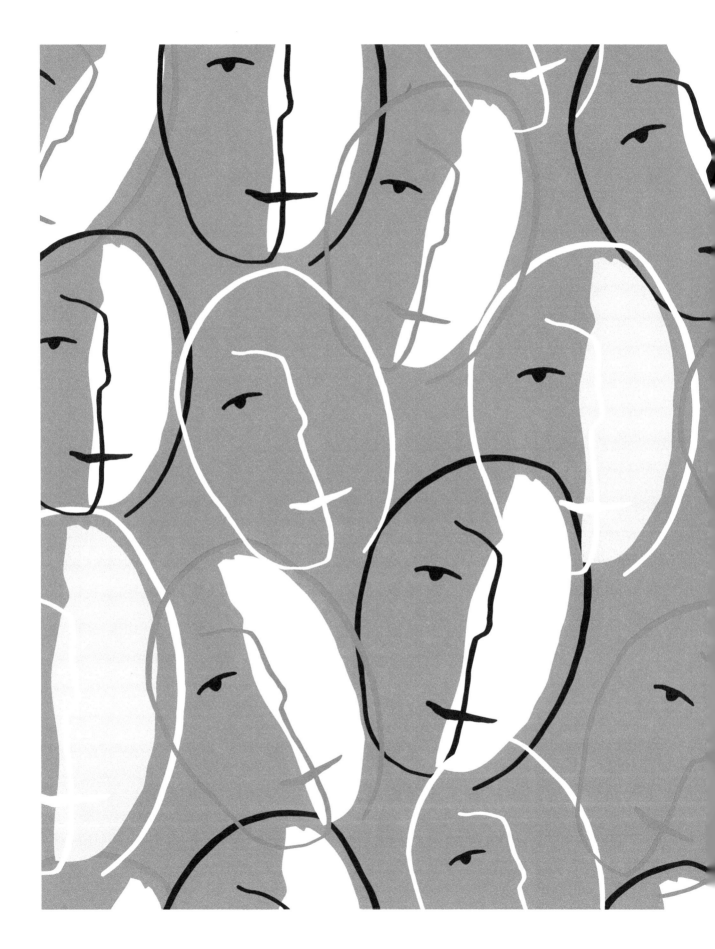

CHAPTER 7

Healthy Relationships

Healthy relationships are the foundation of a satisfying, purpose-driven, and connected life. Children learn to trust others, regulate their emotions, and interact with the world through relationships with important attachment figures. These relationships help them develop a sense of the world as safe or unsafe, and come to understand their own value as individuals. Our brain development in infancy and early childhood is experience dependent; in other words, we develop in response to our relationships with caregivers.

We need each other, and that doesn't stop when we are grown. We are built to be social creatures and to rely on each other throughout our lives. While there is an emphasis on independence and self-sufficiency in our culture, I believe interdependence is a more appropriate expectation for ourselves. Interdependence is the ability to live in harmony and collaboration with others, and to have community and family. Interdependence means we can function independently, and have the wisdom and self-esteem to depend on each other. In a healthy and interdependent relationship, our lives become intertwined, but we take responsibility for our own thoughts, feelings, and behaviors.

Healthy relationships are important to our development, survival, and satisfaction with our lives. In this chapter, we explore what defines healthy relationships, and practice the skills that support us in establishing and maintaining them. Healthy relationships take time and effort.

Defining Healthy Relationship Attributes

What words come to your mind when discussing healthy relationships?

Circle and rate, on a scale of 1 to 5, your top five relationship attributes, with 1 being the most important.

trust	admiring	open communication
respectful	unconditional acceptance	teamwork
reciprocal	shared history	positive regard
fun	safe	benefit of the doubt
playful	kind	accepting
known	tender	positive
understood	vulnerable	intimate
secure	appreciated	forgiving
heard	compromise	
supportive		

Personal Qualities

Whether a romantic relationship, a friendship, or a work relationship, take some time to identify your aspirations for your present and future relationships.

Using your top five from the previous exercise, reflect on the personal qualities each person needs to possess to cultivate the relationship attributes you ranked. For example, trust = honesty, directness in communication, following through on commitments; teamwork = reliable, consistent, responsible, and so on.

_____

_____

_____

_____

_____

_____

_____

_____

_____

QUALITIES TO SEEK IN OTHERS

This is the beginning of constructing what you look for in a future partner, colleague, supervisor, or friend. Look back at chapter 4 where you explored friendship in terms of self-compassion, and review your answers to those questions (see page 54). Using the following list, check the qualities you are looking for in the people you have relationships with.

- [ ] honesty
- [ ] accountability
- [ ] maturity
- [ ] flexibility
- [ ] open-mindedness
- [ ] kindness to strangers
- [ ] self-discipline
- [ ] follow-through/dependability
- [ ] sense of humor
- [ ] ability to self-reflect

- [ ] patience
- [ ] respect for self
- [ ] respect for others
- [ ] living in alignment with values
- [ ] integrity
- [ ] willingness to share history
- [ ] ability to regulate emotions
- [ ] good self-care
- [ ] positive outlook
- [ ] confidence/assertiveness

Coregulating Emotions in Relationships

When we are infants, our nervous systems depend on our caregivers to make us feel safe and connected. Our sense of self develops through the quality of contact we receive from our caregivers. Eye contact, facial expressions, sounds, and touch are the means through which we learned to feel safe and calm or distressed and scared. We learn to regulate our own emotions in this process, as well as how to coregulate emotions with others in relationships.

Coregulation can be defined as one person's autonomic nervous system interacting with another person's system in a way that achieves greater emotional calm. Human beings are deeply connected with each other and influence each other's emotions, sensations, and thoughts. Trauma and abuse can cause difficulties in self-regulating and coregulating, and ongoing emotional dysregulation interferes with our ability to establish and maintain relationships with others.

How we think and feel can change our physiological state, and the ways that we move and breathe can change our thoughts and emotions. This process occurs within us as individuals and in relationships. Listening and witnessing are important parts of establishing and maintaining connection to others. The ability to coregulate in our relationships allows us to feel safe and move into creating and deepening trust and safety. If in our relationships we seek to support each other in achieving a calm, emotional state—even when trying to manage conflict and disagreement—we will continue to feel connected to our partner or significant other.

Exploring Our Relationships

Review the section on values in chapter 5 (see page 80). In those exercises, you identified your personal values and explored how they aligned with the life you have been leading. Now use that same information to look at the people in your life, especially those in your inner circles from the chapter 5 exercise (see page 84). Write and reflect on those relationships. Keep in mind that we are not looking for perfect people, and recovery does not seek perfection from self or others.

> **Are you in relationships with like-minded people who love and support you? Name and reflect on each of those inner-circle relationships.**

_____

_____

_____

_____

_____

_____

_____

_____

_____

_____

Reflection on Past, Present, and Future Relationships

By now you have done a lot of reflecting on your abusive relationship and the other relationships in your life. Hopefully, you are now looking to the future of your relationships as well. I want to invite you to take some time here to reflect on all the exercises you have completed in this workbook so far.

Let's try to integrate some of this material by answering the following questions. I encourage you to take some time with this, as the purpose is to increase your insight and understanding of the past, while generating aspirations for the future.

What have been your primary obstacles to healthy relationships?

_____

_____

_____

_____

_____

_____

_____

_____

What personal qualities do you value in yourself that will help you create and maintain healthy relationships in your life?

_____

_____

_____

_____

_____

_____

_____

_____

_____

_____

What personal qualities or tendencies would you like to adapt or change to promote improvement in your relationships?

_____

_____

_____

_____

_____

_____

_____

_____

_____

_____

BUILDING RELATIONSHIP SKILLS

In this section, I explore emotional intelligence, or EI, a concept popularized in the 1990s by psychologist Daniel Goleman. The basic idea of EI—that certain qualities and abilities help us establish, navigate, and maintain personal and professional relationships—is useful for our purposes. The concepts I am borrowing from EI include self-awareness, emotional regulation, empathy, and social skills.

Let's break down each of these areas and practice some of these skills.

Self-Awareness/Emotional Identification

Self-awareness, or emotional identification, is the ability to name and recognize our own emotions. First, a little psychoeducation about emotions versus feelings might help. Emotions are involuntary responses to events and interactions that we experience in our bodies. Feelings are the words we use to explain and describe these sensations we are involuntarily experiencing.

Now take it a step further. As human beings, we seek to understand our emotions and feelings, so we typically give them a reason or attribute them to something. There is much research and some disagreement about the identity of our basic emotions. For simplicity, I have selected nine basic emotions. We could probably agree that under each of these categories we could generate countless more words that describe a more nuanced emotion.

happiness

sadness

fear

anger

disgust

surprise

jealousy

love

guilt

Do you feel you are "in touch" with your emotions? Why or why not?

_____

_____

_____

| Where do you experience each of these emotions in your body?

happiness _____

sadness _____

fear _____

anger _____

disgust _____

surprise _____

jealousy _____

love _____

guilt _____

RECONNECTING WITH EMOTIONS THROUGH MEMORY

If you find yourself having difficulty identifying emotions in your body, try this exercise. For each of the nine emotion words, choose a memory, and close your eyes. Allow the memory to unfold, and just notice the bodily sensations that accompany that memory. Note them on the previous lines as accurately as you can.

It is not uncommon to resist certain emotions or to try to deny or ignore the sensations in our bodies. Basically we tend to avoid that which we experience as unpleasant. However, emotions serve an important function for us as human beings. They give us information about the world around us and about our relationships. If we ignore, deny, or minimize our emotions, we cut ourselves off from a vital source of information.

In the next section we focus on regulating our emotions. Notice that I said regulate, not control. Remember that our emotions are involuntary—we can't control them. During this exercise, allow your emotions to pass through you, and release them with long, deep breaths.

EMOTIONAL REGULATION

Emotional regulation is the ability to calm ourselves or manage our strong emotions. It is an important skill, because when we have a strong emotion, we typically experience a strong impulse to act.

We want to practice emotional regulation strategies or coping skills in the space between experiencing the emotion and acting on it. This is because we do not make our best decisions when we are experiencing strong emotions, and if we are in a "fight, flight, or freeze" state, it may be difficult for us to manage our reactions.

The fight-or-flight response is triggered involuntarily when we feel threatened. It helps our body prepare to protect itself from a perceived threat. While this response might protect us if we are being chased by a wild animal, it does not serve us if we are required to make a presentation at school or work. Deep breathing, progressive muscle relaxation, distraction, and grounding techniques are all skill categories we can practice to regulate our emotions. I encourage you to experiment with a variety of coping skills to see what seems most helpful.

Here is a partial list of coping skills to practice.

Emotional Regulation Strategies/Coping Skills

Distraction
- Watch a movie.
- Call a friend.
- Color a mandala.
- Journal.
- Do a puzzle.
- Play a game.

Grounding—use your senses to "ground" you in the here and now
- Drink some tea.
- Name 10 things in your surroundings.
- Listen to music.
- Savor some chocolate.
- Exercise.
- Use oils or incense for aromatherapy.
- Take a shower or bath.
- Pet an animal friend.

Deep breathing/relaxation
- Practice diaphragmatic breathing, as introduced in chapter 4 (see page 63).
- Practice progressive muscle relaxation, as introduced in chapter 4 (see page 62).

Thought challenging
- Write down your negative thoughts and challenge their validity.

Spiritual practice
- Meditate.
- Pray.
- Volunteer for a cause.

EMPATHY

Empathy is simply the ability to put yourself in someone else's shoes. It is the ability to sense, recognize, imagine, and understand how another person is feeling. We can cultivate empathy through the practice of particular social engagement skills and by educating ourselves about the lives of people who are different from ourselves.

SOCIAL SKILLS

Social skills encompass using the previous three concepts to guide our pro-social behaviors—actions intended to help others and society. These include:

- Be intentional. Stay focused on what you hope to accomplish in the interaction.
- Be clear. Say what you mean, mean what you say.
- Identify your feelings. Let others know how you feel to help clarify your purpose. Use "I" statements as introduced in chapter 5 (see page 86).
- Practice active listening. Check for meaning and ask clarifying questions.
- Consider your body language and nonverbal communication.
- Attend to the body language and nonverbal communication of others.
- Validate the feelings of others. Let people know you understand their emotional reactions, which goes a long way in de-escalating potential conflicts.
- Avoid criticism and personal attacks.

- Remove yourself from a situation where you are being personally attacked. Taking a time-out is preferable to potentially escalating a situation or allowing yourself to be insulted, abused, or victimized.
- Stick to your values. Don't engage in hate speech and gossip. It is toxic.
- Be honest.
- Practice use of polite words. Say please and thank you.
- Be considerate of others' time. Be aware of your surroundings and the needs of others.
- Negotiate when appropriate, but also practice boundaries.
- Practice recognizing nonverbal communication.

Myths about Expressing Emotions

What myths about emotional expression have kept you from letting others know how you really feel? Check the boxes that apply to you from the following list:

☐ I need to control my emotions.

☐ Expressing emotions is weak.

☐ Only certain emotions are okay.

☐ If I let go and feel this emotion, I will become overwhelmed by it.

☐ If I tell anyone what I feel, they will use it against me.

☐ There must be something wrong with me. Other people don't feel this way.

☐ I should be able to cope without needing support.

☐ People won't like me if I express what I feel.

☐ Being an adult means not having emotional reactions.

☐ Expressing and feeling negative emotions are signs of self-pity.

☐ I need to be rational.

☐ Feelings are irrelevant.

☐ I will look like a drama queen if I express my emotions.

MANAGING CONFLICT IN RELATIONSHIPS

Conflict is inevitable in every relationship. There are good ways and bad ways to navigate conflict, as you know. Avoidance of conflict may be your go-to method because of the way your abuser responded to any efforts you made to express or advocate for yourself.

Understanding how to manage conflict in a healthy way is crucial to move forward. In the previous section, we looked at social skills that support positive healthy relationships, and those apply here as well. Conflict may still seem scary to you because of your experiences, but it doesn't have to be. Setting ground rules with a new partner or simply stating your expectations with others can help tremendously when conflict arises.

In his book *The 7 Habits of Highly Effective People,* Stephen Covey identifies strategies that can be useful and effective in navigating relationships, conflict, or both. The "win-win" and "seek first to understand, then to be understood" concepts are unique approaches to personal conflict.

The win-win strategy means identifying solutions that meet the needs of both parties. It means generating collaborative and mutually beneficial ideas. Just adopting that attitude changes the way we think about conflict. In the "seek first to understand . . ." approach, we practice active listening and empathy. It changes our feelings about the person we are in conflict with and creates an atmosphere of open-mindedness and collaboration.

FAIR FIGHTING RULES

- Don't use insults or name-calling.
- No yelling.
- Stick to the issue at hand. Don't bring up the past.
- Don't use the words "always" and "never."
- Use "I" statements.
- Identify and take responsibility for your feelings. Don't assume or accuse the other person of making you feel a particular way.
- Take turns talking.
- Don't stonewall—shut down or ignore the other person. This does not promote cooperation or compromise.

- Take a time-out if conversation gets heated.
- Allow the other person to take a time-out to cool down. Practice self-regulation if you feel anxious in separating.
- Focus on compromise and solutions instead of fault and blame.

Fighting Fair Reflection

Reflect on these rules. Write any thoughts or feelings you experience when reading through them, and keep your relationships past and present in mind. Do you currently practice these guidelines? In which relationships?

_____

_____

_____

_____

_____

_____

_____

_____

_____

_____

_____

_____

_____

_____

_____

What sensitivities or triggers do you experience in conflict with others as a result of your abusive relationship?

_____

_____

_____

_____

_____

_____

_____

_____

Based on your responses to the last two exercises, add your own rules to the list.

_____

_____

_____

_____

_____

_____

_____

_____

Obstacles to Communication

Look at the following list of obstacles to communication, and checkmark the ones you have used in the last 30 days. Then answer the questions that follow.

☐ **Mind reading:** You expect your partner to know what you're thinking, or you think you know what they "really mean" by what they say.

☐ **Assuming without checking for accuracy:** If we don't ask, we don't know for sure.

☐ **Waiting to talk instead of listening:** If all we are doing is rehearsing our answer, we are not listening attentively to the other person.

☐ **Cherry-picking and filtering:** When we only listen for proof that we are right and ignore other information, we cannot identify common ground.

☐ **Managing stress through conflict:** We argue and debate to blow off steam. If you've been in an abusive relationship, you may be habituated to the cycle of violence.

☐ **Advice-giving:** As soon as the other person raises an issue, we jump in with advice.

☐ **Judging:** We judge the other person, so we cannot really hear their point of view.

☐ **Being right:** We want to be right, so we cannot fully attend to the other's point of view.

☐ **Using humor in a serious conversation:** There are times when lightening the mood is appropriate; however, it can be insensitive when someone wants to be heard and understood.

☐ **Appeasing:** Agreeing just to agree or to end the conversation, not because you actually agree; even going as far as to apologize without any intention of changing behavior.

☐ **Spacing out:** Not paying attention to what the other person is saying may be a way to avoid conflict.

Reflection on My Obstacles

Do you have a preferred obstacle—one that you use more frequently than others?

_____

_____

_____

How do you think that developed?

_____

_____

_____

_____

Are there particular people or an individual that this is more likely to happen with? Explain.

_____

_____

_____

_____

Why might that be?

_____

_____

_____

_____

Are there particular topics that are more difficult for you to communicate about?

_____

_____

_____

_____

Why might that be?

_____

_____

_____

_____

INVESTING IN OUR RELATIONSHIP

Relationships need nurturing to flourish. Focused time, attention, consideration, fun, intimacy, and support are all essential elements to creating and maintaining a healthy relationship. There are no shortcuts here; it takes work and commitment.

- **Create rituals in your relationships.** Whether it's a partner, child, friend, or coworker, traditions and rituals bond us to one another. These don't have to be elaborate. It can be as simple as having breakfast together every Sunday morning, or spending time every evening washing dishes while discussing your day.

- **Celebrate successes together.** Take time to acknowledge each other's successes and accomplishments.

- **Notice and express gratitude to each other.** Take time to acknowledge the efforts of your loved ones.

CHAPTER WRAP-UP

After the pain and loss associated with an abusive relationship, many people may shy away from relationships for a time period because they are too afraid to take this risk again. But I assure you, healthy relationships are possible. In completing this chapter, you have already taken the first steps to creating a new blueprint for your future. This chapter prepared you to define the qualities you desire in current and future relationships. To accomplish this, we focused on qualities to look for in others and qualities you would like to develop or emphasize in yourself. We highlighted key relationship skills, and more specifically, the ability to self-regulate, use coping strategies, identify obstacles to listening, practice empathy, and build pro-social relational strategies. Last, we identified the ability to manage conflict and nurture our relationships as fundamental to achieving and maintaining satisfying, supportive partnerships.

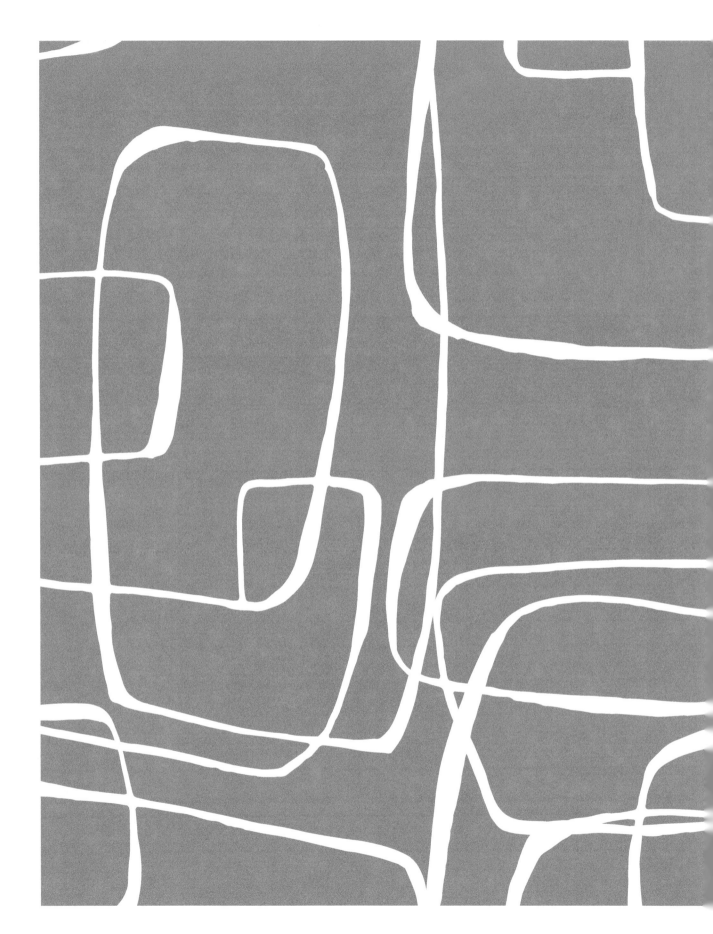

CHAPTER 8

An Exit Plan

The decision to leave a relationship, whether with a lover, friend, family member, or a job, is a difficult and often painful one. You may feel you have lost a part of yourself because of the abuse you've suffered. In previous chapters, we discussed the grief and loss you will experience when making these changes, but you are also likely to experience some anxieties and fears about the future.

It makes sense to plot your course before taking your final exit. Let's begin by exploring your fears and concerns about separating yourself from this situation. Answer the following question:

What difficulties do you anticipate in exiting your abusive relationship/situation?

_____

_____

_____

_____

_____

_____

_____

_____

_____

_____

Exploring Obstacles to Leaving

Remember, if you fear you are in any danger when you leave the relationship, return to review chapter 6 on safety planning and reach out to your local domestic violence agency.

Will leaving your situation affect any of the following categories? Check the boxes beside areas of your life that will be affected.

☐ housing

☐ legal

☐ transportation

☐ health care

☐ financial

☐ support system

☐ employment

Once you have identified your priorities for exiting, you can start taking steps to make the changes you need to leave the abuse behind and move forward. Even if it becomes evident that it may take some time to remove yourself from this situation, it can be very empowering just to take the first few steps toward your independence.

Let's take the list item by item.

Is your housing in jeopardy if you make this move? How so?

_____

_____

_____

_____

Many states have laws regarding breaking your lease if you are in an abusive relationship. Contact your local domestic violence agency for information about this. If you will have difficulty affording housing, consider reaching out to friends, family, and the religious community to see who might be willing to help or knows someone who can. Also, most cities have a housing commission that provides programs and resources for affordable housing. And most cities also have housing resources for victims of domestic abuse—the abuse does not have to be physical to qualify—including short- and some longer-term options, such as shelters and transitional housing. Many faith-based agencies can provide financial assistance with rental deposits or first month's rent, often regardless of whether you are a member of the community. Explore what resources are available in your town or city.

Will your access to transportation be affected by your exit? How so?

_____

_____

_____

_____

Again, you may be surprised to find that nonprofits, faith-based agencies, churches, and domestic violence services sometimes have resources for a variety of needs. Character-based car loans and financial assistance with public transportation are just a couple of possibilities. Traveler's aid also assists with transportation costs if you need to leave town.

Will you be significantly financially affected by your exit? How so?

_____

_____

_____

_____

_____

Making a budget is always a good decision, but it is especially important if you are going to be financially affected by your exit. Start saving as much as you can, as soon as you can, in preparation for this exit. Then look at your monthly bills and income. Is there room to make spending cuts? Do you have the option of getting a side gig for a time? Are there items of value that you can and are willing to sell? Sometimes we feel attached to certain belongings; however, choosing between a possession and being abused might make the decision easier, if not less painful.

If you are leaving a job because of abuse, investigate unemployment compensation. While you are typically not eligible if you quit a job, victimization by a supervisor can be an exception. If you have experienced a high level of stress, depression, or anxiety, taking a medical or family leave may be another option. Check with your HR department and your health care provider. Your provider will typically need to provide some documentation of your condition.

Will your employment be significantly affected by your exit? How so?

_____

_____

_____

_____

_____

Whether it's an abusive boss, family member, or partner connected to your place of employment, you may need to change jobs or at least check out your options to do so. You may be able to use a leave of absence, sick leave, or vacation time to explore other employment options. Update your résumé, and reach out to any contacts you might have. Let the people in your life know what's happening. I have found that many people are willing to help with job leads or career support if they know you are in trouble. Access your personal support system, and look into professional help as well.

Do you need access to legal help? What for and what kind?

_____

_____

_____

_____

_____

Most towns and cities have legal aid and modest means attorneys. Again, if you are exiting an abusive intimate relationship, many domestic violence programs offer consultations with attorneys at low or no cost. Check out your city or town for a Family Justice Center. If you are leaving an abusive intimate relationship, they are a one-stop shop for supportive services, including legal representation.

If you have been abused in the work environment illegally, such as sexual harassment or discrimination, you may find an attorney who is willing to take your case without any money up front, especially if there are other victims.

If you are planning on a legal separation or divorce, speak to a lawyer before you make any decisions. Many lawyers don't advertise this, but are willing to offer an initial consultation for free.

Will your health care be affected by this exit? How so?

_____

_____

_____

_____

_____

If you will lose access to your health care, researching your options will be important here. Most employers offer a COBRA plan, which means you can continue your coverage but you will need to pay for it instead of your employer. Depending on your age, you may be able to get on a family member's plan. Programs vary from state to state, but most states have a marketplace to buy coverage. There are income-based state and federal programs available for low-income families, plus Medicare and Medicaid.

Is your support system affected by this exit? How so?

_____

_____

_____

_____

If you anticipate losing access to your support system, don't hesitate to connect to professional resources. Nonprofits, domestic violence programs, and faith-based organizations and religious communities offer a variety of emotional support services, including counseling, case management, and support groups. There is help available, so don't go it alone.

Look back over the previous exercises in this workbook. Hopefully, you have begun the process of rediscovering yourself and starting to set goals for your future. Recovering from abuse is a difficult and painful process, but you have much to look forward to. The healing process takes so much effort, endurance, and perseverance. Be proud of yourself. You are resilient, or you wouldn't be here.

Strategies for Managing Bullying in the Workplace

When your supervisor is emotionally abusive, it robs you and your coworkers of satisfaction from your work, and adds a level of stress, anxiety, and fear to your daily life. This stress, sense of powerlessness, and anxiety will typically also infiltrate your personal life. If you are in this situation currently, keep these tips in mind:

- Avoid the abuser when it is possible to do so. Notice the warning signs, and when this person is in a "bad mood," try to avoid contact if possible.
- Set boundaries. Saying no to impossible tasks and unreasonable demands in an assertive way can help you feel empowered and may even discourage the bully in your workplace.
- Speak to your coworkers. Enlisting support from others and finding out if they are affected by this behavior also can help you cope and find resources.
- Speak to your human resources department. HR will listen, but they do not always take action. This is especially true if the supervisor is effective in some aspect of their job or for another reason that may or may not be obvious to you. As with other forms of emotional abuse, the behavior is often not illegal, and so it is tolerated.

Your HR department may be able to help you identify options within your workplace, whether to file a complaint, transfer, or take a stress leave. Many workplaces offer Employee Assistance Programs (EAP), which include counseling and sometimes legal or financial advice. Make use of the EAP benefit if it is available. It can help you decide what work and career options exist for you.

What Is Resiliency?

Resiliency is the capacity to bounce back from adversity. We can cultivate resiliency in ourselves. The following is a list of aspects of resiliency:

Relationships: sociability/ability to be a friend, ability to form positive relationships

Service: giving of yourself to help other people, animals, organizations, and/or social causes

Humor: having and using a good sense of humor

Inner Direction: basing choices and decisions on internal evaluation, or internal locus of control

Perceptiveness: insightful understanding of people and situations

Independence: "adaptive" distancing from unhealthy people and situations, autonomy

Flexibility: can adjust to change, can bend as necessary to positively cope with situations

Love of Learning: capacity for and connection to learning

Self-Motivation: internal initiative and positive motivation from within

Competence: being "good at something," personal competence

Self-Worth: feelings of self-worth and self-confidence

Spirituality: personal faith in something greater

Perseverance: continuing on despite difficulty, not giving up

Creativity: expressing yourself through artistic endeavor or through other means of creativity

CHAPTER WRAP-UP

In this chapter, we worked on devising a comprehensive plan for leaving an emotionally abusive situation. Plotting the course of your future beyond abuse can help ensure a successful transition out of these circumstances and minimize the fear that can lead to relapse. The exercises you worked through prepared you for future obstacles and identified varying aspects of necessity moving forward. You also had the opportunity to review potential resources for essentials such as housing, health care, transportation and support systems. In the latter part of the chapter, we highlighted strategies to manage bullying in the workplace. Lastly, we discussed resiliency—if you've made it to this point, you are resilient. Highlighting this strength and other positive qualities can reinforce your commitment to personal growth. When leaving emotionally abusive situations, self-love and the ability to nurture your spirit are key. Embracing your resiliency gives you the knowledge and power needed to survive any difficulties you may face, ultimately creating a future free of abuse.

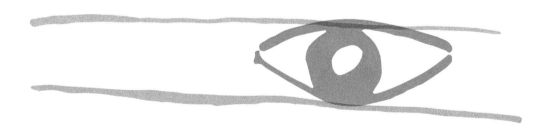

A FINAL WORD

YOU HAVE COME A LONG WAY. You have endured a lot, and completing this workbook shows that you are committed to your own recovery. Be proud of your accomplishments and congratulate yourself for continuing to move forward. There were probably times you wanted to give up, but you didn't, and you likely did all of this while juggling many other responsibilities in your life.

You had the courage to look at your life, yourself, and your pain. Excavating history is a difficult task, but the results can be life-changing. Looking backward to go forward makes sense, and I hope that has been your experience in completing the activities in this book. Once we understand where we've been and how we got there, our choices become clearer and our paths forward become more intentional.

I invite you to take some time to reflect on your experience of completing this workbook. What are the big and small lessons you've discovered on your journey? What might you like to pass on to others? What meaning have you created from this experience?

No matter what responses these questions may prompt, I'm proud of you.

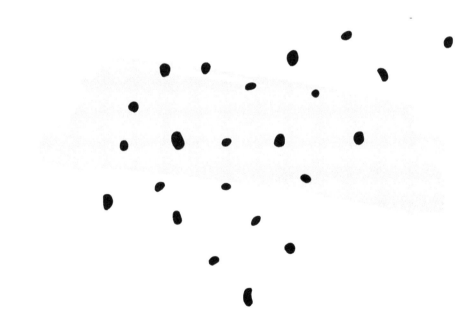

Resources

WEBSITES

BENEFITS.GOV
An official website of the US government that provides web-based benefit information

CODA.ORG
The official website for Co-Dependents Anonymous, a recovery program in the 12-step tradition

HOTPEACHPAGES.NET
An international directory of domestic violence services

JOINONELOVE.ORG
A website that seeks to educate young people about healthy relationships

LOVEISRESPECT.ORG
This support line engages, educates, and empowers young people to prevent and end abusive relationships; free and confidential phone, live chat, and texting services are available 24/7/365:

Chat at www.loveisrespect.org
Text LOVEIS to 1-866-331-9474
Call 1-866-331-9474

NATIONAL DOMESTIC VIOLENCE HOTLINE
Log on to thehotline.org, call 1 (800) 799-7233, 1 (800) 787-3224 TTY, or text LOVEIS to 1-866-331-9474; provides victim/survivor support 24/7

NATIONAL SEXUAL ASSAULT HOTLINE
1 (800) 656-HOPE

NNEDV.ORG
The National Network to End Domestic Violence is dedicated to creating a social, political, and economic environment in which violence against women no longer exists; information and links to other resources

ONLINEPARENTINGPROGRAMS.COM
Information and classes for a variety of topics, including high-conflict divorce, custody, and domestic violence; fee for classes

TECHSAFETY.ORG

A website that offers a tool kit for the safe use of technology in the context of intimate partner abuse, sexual assault, and violence against women

WOMENSHEALTH.GOV

The website of the Office on Women's Health provides a resource line and addresses women's health issues by advancing policies, educating health care professionals and consumers, and supporting programs for women

WOMENSLAW.ORG

A website that provides information relevant to people of all genders, not just women; their email hotline provides legal information to anyone who reaches out with questions regarding domestic violence, sexual violence, or any other covered topic

WORKPLACESRESPOND.ORG

A national hub for information and resources for harassment in the workplace

BOOKS

Splitting: Protecting Yourself While Divorcing Someone with Borderline or Narcissistic Personality Disorder, by Bill Eddy, LCSW, JD, and Randi Kreger

The Verbally Abusive Relationship, by Patricia Evans

References

American Psychiatric Association. *Diagnostic and Statistical Manual of Mental Disorders, Fifth Edition.* Arlington, Virginia: American Psychiatric Publishing, 2013.

Anderson, Kim M. *Enhancing Resilience in Survivors of Family Violence.* New York: Springer Publishing, 2009.

Anderson, Kim M., Lynette M. Renner, and Fran S. Danis. "Recovery: Resilience and Growth in the Aftermath of Domestic Violence." *Violence Against Women* 18, no. 11 (2012): 1279–1299. doi: 10.1177/1077801212470543.

Arabi, Shahida. "The Differences Between Abusers with Narcissistic Personality Disorder vs. Borderline Personality Disorder." Accessed March 22, 2020. Psychcentral.com/lib/the-differences-between-abusers-with-narcissistic-personality-disorder-vs-borderline-personality-disorder.

Baer, Ruth A., Emily L. B. Lykins, and Jessica R. Peters. "Mindfulness and Self-Compassion as Predictors of Psychological Wellbeing in Long-Term Meditators and Matched Nonmeditators." *The Journal of Positive Psychology* 7, no. 3 (May 2012): 230–238. doi:10.1080/17439760.2012.674548.

Brown, David R., and Mark S. Parrish. *College Student Spirituality: Helping Explore Life's Existential Questions.* VISTAS, 2011.

Campbell, Jacquelyn C., ed. *Assessing Dangerousness: Violence by Batterers and Child Abusers. 2nd ed.* New York: Springer Publishing, 2007.

Cloud, Henry, and John Townsend. *Boundaries: When to Say Yes, How to Say No to Take Control of Your Life.* Grand Rapids, Michigan: Zondervan, 1992.

Co-Dependents Anonymous International. "Patterns and Characteristics of Codependence." Accessed March 2020. Coda.org/meeting-materials/patterns-and-characteristics-2011.

Comaford, Christine. "75% of Workers Are Affected by Bullying—Here's What to Do About It." Accessed April 20, 2020. Forbes.com/sites/christinecomaford /2016/08/27/the-enormous-toll -workplace-bullying-takes-on -your-bottom-line/#a223c615595e.

Covey, Stephen. *The 7 Habits of Highly Effective People.* New York: Free Press, 1994.

Doran, G. T. "There's a S.M.A.R.T. Way to Write Management's Goals and Objectives." *Management Review* 70, no. 11 (1981): 35–36.

Goleman, Daniel. *Emotional Intelligence.* New York: Bantam Books, 1995.

Kanter, Jeremy B., and David G. Schramm. "Brief Interventions for Couples: An Integrative Review." *Family Relations* 67 (April 2018): 211–226. doi:10.1111/fare.12298.

Karakurt, G., and K. E. Silver. "Emotional Abuse in Intimate Relationships: The Role of Gender and Age." *Violence and Victims* 28, no. 5 (2013): 804–821. doi. org/10.1891/0886-6708.vv-d-12-00041.

McKay, Matthew, Patrick Fanning, and Kim Paleg. *Couple Skills. 2nd ed.* Oakland, California: New Harbinger Publications, 2006.

Mulay, A. L., M. H. Waugh, J. P. Fillauer, D. S. Bender, A. Bram, N. M. Cain, E. Caligor, et al. "Borderline Personality Disorder Diagnosis in a New Key." *Borderline Personality Disorder and Emotion Dysregulation* 6, no. 18 (2019). doi.org/10.1186/s40479-019-0116-1.

Naparstek, Belleruth. *Invisible Heroes: Survivors of Trauma and How They Heal.* New York: Bantam Dell, 2006.

Neff, K. D. "The Science of Self-Compassion," in *Wisdom and Compassion in Psychotherapy: Deepening Mindfulness in Clinical Practice,* edited by C. K. Germer and R. D. Siegel, 79–92. New York: Guilford Press, 2012.

Novotney, Amy. *"The Risks of Social Isolation."* American Psychological Association 50, no. 5 (May 2019). http://apa.org/monitor/2019/05/ce -corner-isolation.

Peterson, Joann S. *Anger, Boundaries and Safety.* Gabriola Island, BC, Canada: PD Publishing, 2001.

Proeve, Michael, Rebekah Anton, and Maura Kenny. "Effects of Mindfulness-Based Cognitive Therapy on Shame, Self-Compassion and Psychological Distress in Anxious and Depressed Patients: A Pilot Study." *Psychology and Psychotherapy: Theory, Research and Practice* 91 (2018): 434–449. doi:10.1111/papt.12170.

Salovey, Peter, Marc A. Brackett, and John D. Mayer. *Emotional Intelligence.* Port Chester, NY: Dude Publishing, 2004.

SAMHSA Native Connections. "Setting Goals and Developing Specific, Measurable, Achievable, Relevant, and Time-bound Objectives" (PDF). Substance Abuse and Mental Health Services Administration. samhsa.gov/sites/default/files/nc-smart-goals-fact-sheet.pdf.

Ureña, Julissa, Eva M. Romera, Jose A. Casas, Carmen Viejo, and Rosario Ortega-Ruiz. "Psichometrics Properties of Psychological Dating Violence Questionnaire: A Study with Young Couples." *International Journal of Clinical and Health Psychology* 15 (2015): 52–60. dx.doi.org/10.1016/j.ijchp.2014.07.002.

Van Der Kolk, Bessel. *The Body Keeps the Score.* New York: Penguin, 2015.

Warshaw, Carole, Phyllis Brashler, and Jessica Gil. "Mental Health Consequences of Intimate Partner Violence," in *Intimate Partner Violence: A Health-Based Perspective,* edited by Connie Mitchell, 147–172. New York: Oxford University Press, 2009. nationalcenterdvtraumamh.org/wp-content/uploads/2015/10/Mitchell-Chapter-12.pdf.

Zhang, Huaiyu, Natalie N. Watson-Singleton, Sara E. Pollard, Delishia M. Pittman, Dorian A. Lamis, et al. "Self-Criticism and Depressive Symptoms: Mediating Role of Self-Compassion." *Journal of Death and Dying* 80, no. 2 (September 2017): 202–223. doi:10.1177/0030222817729609.

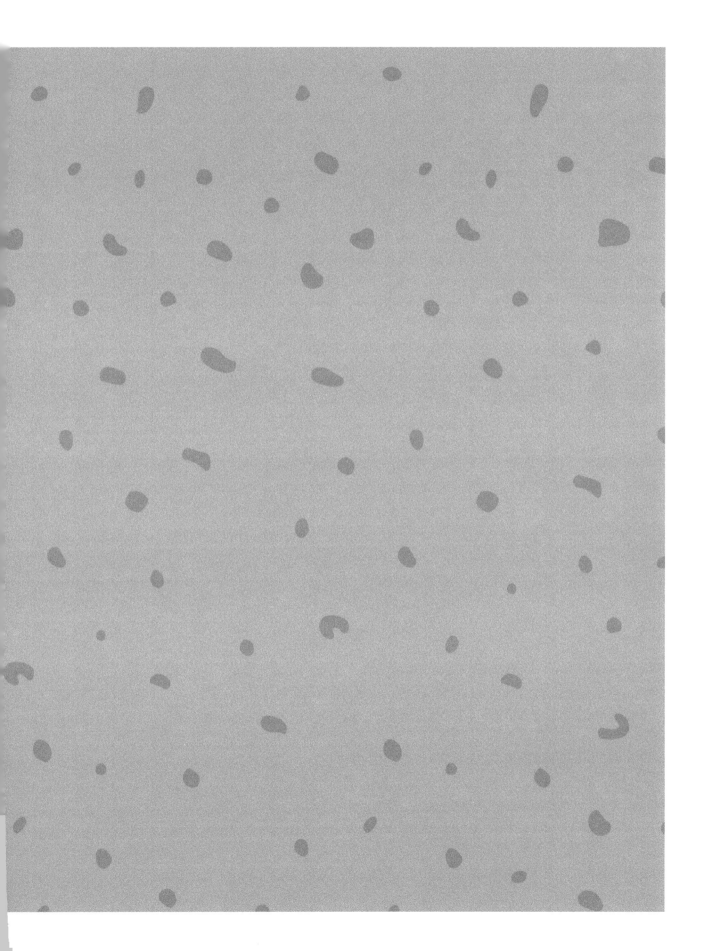

Index

N

Name-calling, 4–5

Narcissistic personality disorder (NPD), 16

Needs, 69

Neff, Kristin, 53

Neglect, 7

P

Personal protection orders, 102

Progressive muscle relaxation, 62–63

Psychological violence, 3

Punishment, 7

R

"Red flags," 4

Rejecting behavior, 7

Relationships
    healthy, 107–109
    history, 46–48
    investing in, 125
    managing conflict in, 119–124
    qualities to seek in others, 109–112
    skills, 113–118

Resiliency, 134

Responsibility, taking, 14

Restraining orders, 102

Ripple effects, 30

Rituals, grief, 32

S

Safety plans, 93–103

Schedules, 69

Self-awareness, 114–115

Self-care, 64–71

Self-compassion, 53–60, 71

7 Habits of Highly Effective People, The (Covey), 119

Shaming, 18–19

Sleep hygiene, 67

SMART goals, 70–71, 98

Social skills, 117–118

Social withdrawal, 10

Spirituality, 65, 135

Support networks, 128–132

Survival mode, 51

T

Therapist, ix

Threats, 6–7

V

Values, 80–85

Vanity, 15

Victim-playing, 15

Vulnerability, 11–12

W

Weather metaphor, 60–61

Workplace
    bullying in, 133
    exit plans, 130–132

Y

Yelling, 5

About the Author

Theresa Comito, LMFT, is a licensed marriage and family therapist in California with more than 20 years of experience providing therapeutic services to individuals, families, and children, and 28 years in nonprofit settings. Theresa's work has served families fleeing domestic violence, victims of crime, and survivors of abuse and trauma.

Currently, she has a private practice in San Diego, California, and continues to work in the nonprofit sector, providing clinical supervision to graduate students and interns.

CPSIA information can be obtained
at www.ICGtesting.com
Printed in the USA
JSHW020847030920
7413JS00004B/5

9 781647 391843